Basic Knowledge of Gemstones

# 宝石の常識
## International

双葉社

# はじめに Preface

宝石は、母なる地球から私たち人類への大切な贈り物です。

私たちの祖先が今よりも自然と調和しながら生きていた時代、人々は地球の一部である宝石に特別なエネルギーを感じ、その力を活用しながらさまざまなインスピレーションを受け取って生きていました。

時代が下がり研磨技術が発展すると、今度はその類まれなる輝きと美しさが人々を魅了するようになります。私たち人類は長い歴史の中で、さまざまな角度から宝石に魅力を感じ、絶大な価値を見い出してきたのです。

本書『宝石の常識』は、私の師である故・岡本憲将氏（株式会社ベル・エトワール創業者）が1996年に発刊し、その後10冊以上出版された人気シリーズです。その時代ごとに人気のあるカラーストーンを中心に、多数の美しい写真と共にわかりやすく宝石の価値基準や、産地情報、色の違い、そして宝石が秘めるエネルギーの活用方法などを紹介してきました。

2020年発刊の前書より私が監修を引き継ぎ、今回はインターナショナル版として、これまでご要望の多かった英語の対訳を表記しました。宝石がもつ4つの価値を、世界中の皆さんにご紹介できることをとても嬉しく思っています。

光り輝く宝石を活用して、皆さんの心・体・魂もキラキラと輝き、共により良い未来を創ることができましたら幸いです。

Gemstones are precious gifts from Mother Earth to humanity.

In the past, when our ancestors lived in closer harmony with nature, they sensed a special energy in gemstones, seeing them as part of the Earth itself. By harnessing this energy, they found inspiration and incorporated gemstones into their daily lives.

As cutting and polishing techniques advanced over time, people became captivated by the extraordinary brilliance and beauty of gemstones. Throughout history, humanity has admired gemstones from multiple perspectives and attributed great value to them.

This book, *Basic knowledge of Gemstones*, was first published in 1996 by my mentor, the late Mr. Kensho Okamoto, founder of Belle Etoile Co., Ltd. Since then, it has become a popular series, with over 10 editions published. Each edition has focused on the most sought-after colored gemstones of its time, offering clear explanations of valuation criteria, sources, color variations, and even ways to harness the energy that gemstones possess—all accompanied by stunning photographs.

Since the 2020 edition, I have taken over as the supervisor of this series. For this international edition, we have included English translations in response to numerous requests from readers. I am truly delighted to share the four essential values of gemstones with people around the world.

I sincerely hope that by embracing the brilliance of gemstones, your heart, body, and soul will shine ever brighter, and together, we can create a more luminous future.

株式会社ベル・エトワール
代表取締役

## 岡本敬人

Belle Etoile Co., Ltd.
President & CEO: Takahito Okamoto

Profile_

# Takahito Okamoto

President & CEO of
Belle Etoile Co., Ltd. /
Jewelry Energy Advisor

---

岡本敬人

株式会社ベル・エトワール
代表取締役社長／
ジュエリーエネルギーアドバイザー

多くの人を笑顔にしたいという思いのもと音楽活動を行い、1997年にバンドのヴォーカリストとしてメジャーデビュー。音楽業界の第一線で多岐にわたって活躍する。2010年に株式会社ベル・エトワールの創業者であり宝石の伝道師の岡本憲将氏と出会い、宝石が持つ癒しの力に感銘を受け、自身もその価値を多くの人に伝えたいと憲将氏に師事し、2012年にジュエリーエネルギーアドバイザーの資格を取得。これまでに2万人以上の宝石フィッティングを行う。2017年より株式会社ベル・エトワールの代表取締役を引き継ぎ、東京・銀座を拠点に全国でセミナーや体感会を開催。著書に『宝石の常識 永久保存版』（双葉社）、『JEWELLNESS 心と体を癒す宝石の価値』（幻冬舎MC）、『Gemstone 人々を輝かせる宝石の秘密』（幻冬舎MC）がある。

Driven by a passion for bringing joy to people, Mr.Takahito Okamoto first pursued a career in music, making his major debut as a band vocalist in 1997. He thrived in the music industry, engaging in a wide range of creative and professional activities.In 2010, he met Mr. Kensho Okamoto, the founder of Belle Etoile Co., Ltd. and a renowned gemstone evangelist. Deeply moved by the healing energy of gemstones, he decided to study under Mr. Okamoto to share this knowledge with a wider audience. In 2012, he obtained certification as a Jewelry Energy Advisor and has since conducted gemstone fittings for over 20,000 individuals.In 2017, he took over as president & CEO of Belle Etoile Co., Ltd. Based in Ginza, Tokyo, he organizes seminars and experiential gemstone events across Japan.He is also the author of *Basic Knowledge of Gemstones: The Ultimate Guide* (Futabasha Publishers Ltd.), *JEWELLNESS: The Healing Energy of Gemstones* (Gentosha Media Consulting), and *Gemstone: The Secret to Enhancing People's Brilliance* (Gentosha Media Consulting).

# Contents

004　はじめに　文・岡本敬人

**巻頭グラビア**
## 宝石の4つの価値

020　トルマリン
- パライバトルマリン [023]　● ブルートルマリン [025]
- グリーントルマリン [026]　● ルベライト&ピンクトルマリン [027]
- イエロートルマリン [028]　● バイカラートルマリン [029]
- トルマリンキャッアイ [030]
- トルマリンの産出動向とその価値 [031]

034　ガーネット
- デマントイドガーネット [035]　● グリーンガーネット [036]
- カラーチェンジガーネット [037]　● ロードライトガーネット [038]
- マンダリンガーネット&スペッサータイトガーネット [039]
- マリガーネット [040]　● マラヤガーネット [041]
- ドラゴンガーネット [042]
- ガーネットの産出動向とその価値 [044]

050　オパール
- ブラックオパール [052]　● ブラックオパール色の価値基準表 [054]
- ボルダーオパール [056]　● エチオピアオパール [057]
- メキシコオパール [058]　● オパールの産出動向とその価値 [059]

064　サファイア
- ブルーサファイア [065]　● スターサファイア [067]
- ブルーサファイア&スターサファイア 色の価値基準表 [068]
- パパラチアサファイア [070]　● ピンクサファイア [072]
- オレンジサファイア [073]
- ゴールデンサファイア&イエローサファイア [074]
- グリーンサファイア&バイオレットサファイア&
　バイカラーサファイア [075]
- ファンシーカラーサファイア 色の価値基準表 [076]
- サファイアの産出動向とその価値 [078]

080　ルビー
- ルビー [081]　● スタールビー [082]
- ルビーの産出動向とその価値 [083]
- ルビー&スタールビー 色の価値基準表 [084]

086　エメラルド
- エメラルド [087]　● レッドエメラルド　エメラルドキャッツアイ&トラ
ピッチェエメラルド [088]　● エメラルドの産出動向とその価値 [089]
- エメラルド 色の価値基準表 [090]

092　アレキサンドライト
- アレキサンドライト [094]
- アレキサンドライトの産出動向とその価値 [095]
- アレキサンドライト 色の価値基準表 [096]

102　キャッツアイ
- キャッツアイ [103]　● アレキサンドライトキャッツアイ [104]
- キャッツアイの産出動向とその価値 [105]
- キャッツアイ 色の価値基準表 [106]

108　ヒスイ
- ヒスイ [109]　● ラベンダーヒスイ [111]
- ヒスイの産出動向とその価値 [112]
- コラム　縄文人が愛したヒスイ [113]

114　ダイヤモンド
- ダイヤモンド [115]
- ピンクダイヤモンド&イエローダイヤモンド [116]
- ブルーダイヤモンド&グリーンダイヤモンド&
　ブラウンダイヤモンド [117]
- ダイヤモンドの産出動向とその価値 [118]

119　宝石の街 ジャイプール訪問記
文・岡本敬人

122　トパーズ
- インペリアルトパーズ [123]
- ピンクトパーズ&バイカラートパーズ [124]
- トパーズの産出動向とその価値 [125]

126　タンザナイト
- タンザナイト [128]　● タンザナイトの産出動向とその価値 [129]

130　インカローズ
- インカローズ [131]　● インカローズの産出動向とその価値 [132]

**特集**
## セミプレシャスストーン
- アクアマリン [134]　● ペリドット [136]　● スフェーン [138]
- ロイヤルブルームーンストーン [140]　● スファレライト [142]
- クンツァイト [144]　● モルガナイト [145]
- スピネル [146]　● ジルコン [147]

148　レアストーン
- パラサイトペリドット [149]
- ステラエスペランサ [150]
- アウイナイト／グリーンアウイナイト [152]
- ハイアライト／スキャポライト [153]
- キャシテライト／オレゴンサンストーン [154]
- アイドクレース／カイヤナイト [155]
- アパタイト／ベニトアイト [156]
- フローライト／ヴェイリネナイト [157]

## 宝石の4つの価値
- 財産として [158]
- 美しさとして／装飾として [161]
- エネルギーとして [162]
- 宝石エネルギーの伝道師・岡本憲将 [164]
- ドクターと共に宝石のエネルギーを科学的に検証 [165]
- 宝石種別効能リスト [167]
- 自分に合った宝石の見つけ方&ヒーリング方法 [173]
- ヒーリングメソッド [174]
- 宝石のお手入れ方法 [176]

**インタビュー**
- インドの宝石商 サンディープ・ラワット氏 [046]
- オパール輸出卸売業者 蓑田秀一氏 [060]
- ドバイの宝石ディーラー ザヒール・アンサリ氏 [098]

004 **Preface**  by Mr. Takahito Okamoto

008 `Gallery`
# The 4 Values of Gemstones

020 ## Tourmaline
- Paraiba Tourmaline [023]  ● Blue Tourmaline [025]
- Green Tourmaline [026]  ● Rubellite & Pink Tourmaline [027]
- Yellow Tourmaline [028]  ● Bicolor Tourmaline [029]
- Tourmaline Cat's Eye [030]
- Production Trends and Value [031]

034 ## Garnet
- Demantoid Garnet [035]  ● Green Garnet [036]
- Color-Change Garnet [037]  ● Rhodolite Garnet [038]
- Mandarin Garnet & Spessartite Garnet [039]
- Mali Garnet [040]  ● Malaya Garnet [041]
- Dragon Garnet [042]
- Production Trends and Value [044]

050 ## Opal
- Black Opal [052]  ● Black Opal Color Grading Table [054]
- Boulder Opal [056]  ● Ethiopian Opal [057]
- Mexican Opal [058]  ● Production Trends and Value [059]

064 ## Sapphire
- Blue Sapphire [065]  ● Star Sapphire [067]
- Blue Sapphire & Star Sapphire Color Grading Table [068]
- Padparadscha Sapphire [070]  ● Pink Sapphire [072]
- Orange Sapphire [073]
- Golden Sapphire & Yellow Sapphire [074]
- Green Sapphire, Violet Sapphire & Bicolor Sapphire [075]
- Fancy-Colored Sapphire Grading Table [076]
- Production Trends and Value [078]

080 ## Ruby
- Ruby [081]  ● Star Ruby [082]
- Production Trends and Value [083]
- Ruby & Star Ruby Color Grading Table [084]

086 ## Emerald
- Emerald [087]  ● Red Emerald / Emerald Cat's Eye & Trapiche Emerald [088]  ● Production Trends and Value [089]
- Emerald Color Grading Table [090]

092 ## Alexandrite
- Alexandrite [094]
- Production Trends and Value [095]
- Alexandrite Color Grading Table [096]

102 ## Cat's Eye
- Cat's Eye [103]  ● Alexandrite Cat's Eye [104]
- Production Trends and Value [105]
- Cat's Eye Color Grading Table [106]

108 ## Jade
- Jade [109]  ● Lavender Jade [111]
- Production Trends and Value [112]
- Column: Jade: Cherished by Jomon People [113]

114 ## Diamond
- Diamond [115]
- Pink Diamond & Yellow Diamond [116]
- Blue Diamond, Green Diamond & Brown Diamond [117]
- Production Trends and Value [118]

119 ## A Visit to Jaipur, the City of Gems
Text by Takahito Okamoto

122 ## Topaz
- Imperial Topaz [123]
- Pink Topaz & Bicolor Topaz [124]
- Production Trends and Value [125]

126 ## Tanzanite
- Tanzanite [128]  ● Production Trends and Value [129]

130 ## Inca Rose
- Inca Rose [131]  ● Production Trends and Value [132]

133 `Feature`
# Semi-Precious Stones
- Aquamarine [134]  ● Peridot [136]  ● Sphene [138]
- Royal Blue Moonstone [140]  ● Sphalerite [142]
- Kunzite [144]  ● Morganite [145]
- Spinel [146]  ● Zircon [147]

148 # Rare Stones
- Pallasite Peridot [149]
- Stella Esperanza [150]
- Hauynite / Green Hauynite [152]
- Hyalite / Scapolite [153]
- Cassiterite / Oregon Sunstone [154]
- Idocrase / Kyanite [155]
- Apatite / Benitoite [156]
- Fluorite / Vayrynenite [157]

158 # The 4 Values of Gemstones
- As Assets [158]
- As Beauty / As Adornment [161]
- As Energy [162]
- A Leading Voice in Gemstone Energy: Mr. Kensho Okamoto [164]
- Scientific Analysis of Gemstone Energies with Medical Experts [165]
- List of Benefits by Gemstone Type [167]
- Finding Your Perfect Gemstone & Healing Methods [173]
- Healing Methods [174]
- How to Care for Gemstones [176]

`Inerview`
- Indian Gem Dealer: Mr. Sandeep Rawat [046]
- Opal Export and Wholesale Dealer: Mr. Shu Minoda [060]
- Dubai Gem Dealer: Mr. Zaheer Ansari [098]

## *Beauty 1*
# Brilliant Red & Pink

煌びやかな赤とピンク

(Center)
・Pt Ring_Padparadscha Sapphire3.967ct,D3.25ct
(Clockwise from the left)
・Pt Pendant_Inca Rose6.93ct,D1.31ct
・Pt Ring_Ruby6.15ct,D2.63ct
・Kunzite56.88ct
・Morganite48.95ct
・Dragon Garnet19.28ct
・Red Topaz10.78ct

# The 4 Values of Gemstones

― 宝石の4つの価値 ―

― Beauty ―
# 1
# *V*ivid Orange & Yellow
鮮烈なオレンジとイエロー

(From top to bottom)
- Yellow Tourmaline14.84ct
- Orange Sapphire8.51ct
- Spessartite Garnet20.37ct

(From left to right)
- Pt／YG Ring_Golden Sapphire4.55ct,D0.52ct
- Pt Ring_Yellow Sapphire3.70ct,D0.498ct
- Pt Pendant_Imperial Topaz21.92ct,D0.92ct
- Pt Pendant_Sphalerite15.48ct, Morganite1.50ct,D0.90ct

# Beauty 1
## Calm Green
心穏やかな緑

(Clockwise from the top)
- Pt Pendant_Sphene24.68ct,D1.06ct
- Green Tourmaline35.96ct
- Green Garnet10.08ct
- Pt Ring_Cab Emerald6.15ct,D0.60ct
- Pt Ring_Demantoid Garnet2.27ct,D1.42ct

(Clockwise from top left)
· Pt Pendant_Aquamarine23.99ct,D0.47ct
· Pt Pendant_Paraiba Tourmaline5.55ct,D1.53ct
· WG Pendant_Apatite11.63ct
· Stella Esperanza50.51ct
· Blue Sapphire13.14ct
· Pt Ring_Tanzanite20.35ct,D3.37ct

The 4 Values of Gemstones

— Beauty —
1
Striking Blue

衝撃の青

# *The* Magic of Black and Boulder Opals

— Adornment 2 —

ブラック&ボールダーオパールの魔法

- Pt Ring_Black Opal5.58ct,D4.33ct
- Pt/YG Necklace_
 (Opal from left) Black Opal0.46ct,2.32ct,2.23ct,3.13ct,1.55ct,Boulder Opal5.53ct
 (Center) Boulder Opal18.10ct,D7.32ct

The 4 Values of Gemstones

(Clockwise from top left)
- Pt Necklace_Cab Paraiba Tourmaline
- Pt Earrings_Cab Paraiba Tourmaline
- Pt Ring_Paraiba Tourmaline1.17ct,D1.37ct
- Pt Ring_Paraiba Tourmaline1.27ct,D1.40ct

— Adornment 2 —
# Wrapped in Earth's Blue
地球の青に包まれて

(Top)
• Pt Pearl Necklace_Ruby3.05ct,D4.33ct
(Clockwise from top left)
• YG Ring_Imperial Topaz7.78ct,D0.21ct
• YG Ring_Golden Sapphire4.97ct,D1.93ct
• YG Tie Tack_Black Opal5.147ct,D0.18ct
• YG Pendant_Spinel4.93ct

— Adornment —

# Unique Charms of Colors & Shapes

色や形の個性で遊ぶ！

— Adornment —
# Playfulness in your Style–Jewelry for Men

遊び心あふれるメンズジュエリー

(Center)
- Pt／YG Ring_Cat's Eye20.48ct,D4.25ct

(Clockwise from top left)
- YG Pendant_Black Opal7.36ct,D0.72ct
- Pt Ring_Aquamarine5.65ct,D0.50ct
- WG Tie Tack_Inca Rose4.70ct,D1.08ct
- Pt Ring_Emerald4.35ct,D0.465ct
- YG Ring_Tanzanite6.94ct,D1.99ct

The 4 Values of Gemstones

# The 4 Values of Gemstones

- WG Necklace_Orange Sapphire16.09ct,D6.92ct (Clockwise from top)
- Pt Ring_Emerald5.84ct,D2.48ct
- Pt Ring_Blue Sapphire7.48ct,D2.77ct
- Ruby15.47ct

— Assets 3 —

## Timeless Icons: the Three Finest Gemstones

永遠の憧れ世界の三大宝石

(Clockwise from top left)
- Tanzanite 73.14ct
- Pt Ring_Alexandrite 5.51ct, D3.23ct
- Pt Pendant_Black Opal 8.78ct, D3.39ct
- Pt Ring_Paraiba Tourmaline 5.78ct, D0.39ct
- Paraiba Tourmaline 3.08ct

— Assets —

## 3
# Stones of Noble Majesty

威厳に満ちた高貴な石

# The 4 Values of Gemstones

— Energy —
## Jewels of Joy & Healing
幸せと癒しを呼ぶ宝石

(Clockwise from top left)
- YG Pendant_ (from the top) Yellow Diamond0.26ct,Phenakite3.411ct,Zoisite17.48ct
- Pt Pendant_ (from the top) Hyalite1.55ct,Tanzanite7.361ct,D0.23ct
- Pt／YG Pendant_ (from the top) Pallasite Peridot0.07ct／0.317ct, Imperial Topaz3.92ct, Paraiba Tourmaline8.17ct,D0.64ct
- Pt Pendant_ (from the top) Dragon Garnet0.16ct, Mali Garnet1.54ct, Black Opal5,97ct,D0.63ct

— Energy —

# 4
# *Enjoy the Art of Gem Combinations*

組み合わせて楽しむ宝石

(Clockwise from top left)
- YG Pendant_ （from the top）Pallasite Peridot0.987ct,Black Opal11.60ct,Pallasite Peridot0.062ct
- YG Ring_ （from the top）Star Ruby1.86ct,Cab Emerald2.56ct,Black Opal0.88ct
- WG Pendant_ （from the top）Yellow Diamond0.25ct,Paraiba Tourmaline0.33ct, Imperial Topaz0.69ct, Stella Esperanza11.63ct,D0.31ct
- Pt／YG Pendant_ （from the top）Paraiba Tourmaline0.366ct,Padparadscha Sapphire0.69ct, Green Diamond0.24ct,Green Sapphire1.08ct,Pallasite Peridot0.035ct,Spinel1.58ct,D0.08ct
- YG Pendant_ （from the top）Green Garnet0.25ct,Hyalite0.05ct,Ruby1.12ct,D0.07ct

019

# Tourmaline

トルマリン

**色相、個性ともに豊かな色石**

　青、赤、オレンジ、黄、緑、藍、茶色と、宝石類のなかでも色相が最も豊富なトルマリン。キャッツアイやバイカラーなどもあり、ひとくくりでは捉えきれない多彩な魅力にあふれています。

　色の違いは結晶構造に入る成分によります。マンガンが含まれるとピンクから赤、鉄とチタンでは黄、酸化クロムなら緑、二価鉄、三価鉄では青になります。世界各地で産出されますが、宝石質の原石はごく一部。それぞれの種類で稀少性と色の美しさによって評価は大きく異なります。

**Rich in Color Diversity and Unique Character**

Tourmaline, with its extensive range of colors—blue, red, orange, yellow, green, indigo, and brown—is one of the most color-diverse gemstones. It also features unique characteristics such as cat's eye and bicolor variations, making it a gemstone that cannot be easily categorized.

　The differences in color are determined by the elements incorporated into its crystal structure. For instance, manganese results in pink to red colors, iron and titanium produce yellow, chromium oxide creates green, and divalent or trivalent iron results in blue. Although tourmalines are mined worldwide, only a small fraction of the material is of gem quality. The rarity of each variety and the beauty of its color significantly influence its value.

# Tourmaline

(From the left to right)
- WG Pendant_Green Tourmaline16.24ct,D1.17ct
- Pink Tourmaline 2.68ct
- Pt Ring_Paraiba Tourmaline3.48ct,D3.49ct
- Pt Ring_Cab Rubellite11.88ct,D0.62ct
- Golconda Tourmaline 11.90ct
- Canary Tourmaline 15.57ct
- Bicolor Tourmaline 8.30ct
- Bicolor Tourmaline Cat's eye 6.143ct

## Tourmaline in a Wide Range of Colors

(From top left to bottom)
Indigolite Tourmaline3.18ct, Green Tourmaline3.91ct, Green Tourmaline 1.80ct, Paraiba Tourmaline6.63ct, Paraiba Tourmaline2.20ct, Paraiba Tourmaline 1.24ct, Paraiba Tourmaline1.58ct, Paraiba Tourmaline0.16ct, Paraiba Tourmaline 0.12ct, Rubellite15.48ct, Pink Tourmaline2.52ct, Canary Tourmaline2.79ct, Rubellite2.30ct, Yellow Tourmaline1.53ct, Pink Tourmaline2.75ct, Pink Tourmaline1.41ct, Rubellite1.10ct

(From top left to right)
- Pt Ring_Paraiba Tourmaline4.68ct,D2.65ct
- Pt Ring_Paraiba Tourmaline1.19ct,D0.38ct
- Pt Ring_Paraiba Tourmaline1.44ct,D0.682ct
- Pt Ring_Paraiba Tourmaline2.88ct,D2.94ct
- Paraiba Tourmaline2.33ct
- Paraiba Tourmaline3.63ct

Tourmaline

(From top left to right)
- Pt Ring_Paraiba Tourmaline1.69ct,D0.668ct
- Pt Ring_Paraiba Tourmaline0.99ct,D0.65ct
- Pt Ring_Paraiba Tourmaline1.57ct,PD0.285ct,D4.03ct
- Pt/YG Ring_Paraiba Tourmaline0.708ct,D0.11ct
- Pt Pendant_Paraiba Tourmaline0.14ct,D0.30ct

# Paraiba Tourmaline

パライバトルマリン

## 宝石の美を極限まで高めたネオンブルー

　ブラジルのパライバ州で1989年に発見され、州名にちなんで命名されたパライバトルマリン。色みも個性も多様なトルマリンのなかで、圧倒的な人気と稀少性を誇ります。最大の魅力は、目の覚めるような鮮烈な色。他の色石にはないトロリとしたテリのある青は蛍光色を感じさせ、ネオンブルーと形容されます。宇宙から見た地球の色を彷彿させるとして、「地球の青」とも呼ばれます。

　その独特な色合いは内包された酸化クロムと銅が生み出した奇跡です。通常は反発し合う2つの金属元素が、パライバトルマリンでは混ざり合い、超絶的な美を生み出しています。酸化クロムが強いと青、銅が強いとグリーン系になります。

## Neon Blue: Elevating the Beauty of Gemstones to Its Fullest

Discovered in Brazil's Paraíba state in 1989 and named after the region, the Paraiba tourmaline stands out as one of the most coveted and rare gemstones within the diverse and vibrant family of tourmalines. Its most striking feature is its vivid, electrifying color. The intense, glowing blue—often described as "neon blue"—exudes a unique, liquid-like luster unmatched by other colored gemstones. This exceptional color has earned it the nickname "Earth's Blue," as it resembles the color of our planet as seen from space.

　This extraordinary coloration is the result of a rare combination of chromium oxide and copper within the stone. These two metallic elements, which are not commonly found together, are uniquely found in Paraiba tourmaline, creating its unparalleled beauty. A higher concentration of chromium oxide results in blue tones, while a stronger presence of copper gives the stone a greenish tint.

## 類まれな美しさから大人気に

市場に出回る良質のパライバトルマリンのほとんどは、ブラジルで発見された当初のもの。以降はあまり採れなくなり、続いて発見された他の産地も産出量が少なく、良質なものはわずかです。見る人を魅了する美しさから世界的に爆発的な人気を呼び、稀少性も相まってその価格は20年で100倍以上に高騰したものもあります。

最高級品は蛍光する鮮やかな青で、透明感がありながらテリを伴います。近年一級品の1カラット以上のものは減っており、価格も高騰し続けています。ネオンブルーが評価される一方、トロリとした色合いのグリーンが美しい一級品もあります。内包物は本来なら融合しない元素が生む色だけに多く、美しさを損なわなければ気にする必要はありません。

*(From top to bottom)*
- Pt Ring_Paraiba Tourmaline1.22ct,D0.4ct
- YG Ring_Paraiba Tourmaline1.336ct,D0.36ct
- Paraiba Tourmaline2.12ct

### Renowned for Its Unparalleled Beauty

Most of the high-quality Paraiba tourmalines available on the market today are from the original discoveries in Brazil. Since then, production has significantly declined, and even other subsequently discovered sources have yielded only small quantities, with top-quality stones being exceptionally rare. Their captivating beauty has sparked explosive global popularity, and their rarity has driven prices to skyrocket. In some cases, prices have increased more than 100-fold over the past 20 years.

The finest specimens are characterized by their vivid, fluorescent blue, combining clarity and luster. In recent years, however, the availability of top-grade stones of one carat or more has sharply decreased, and prices continue to soar. While the neon blue variety is highly prized, exceptional stones with a rich green color are also celebrated for their beauty. The inclusions in Paraiba tourmalines, resulting from the combination of elements that rarely coexist, are abundant. However, they are not a concern as long as they do not detract from the gem's overall beauty.

## Color variations

**Blue Type**

**Green Type**

蛍光する鮮やかな青ほど高い評価。ブラジル産の一級品は現在ほぼ産出されず、市場に流通するのは淡い色合いがほとんど。

The more vibrant fluorescent blue colors are highly prized. However, top-quality Paraiba tourmalines from Brazil are now nearly depleted, and most of the stones available on the market today exhibit softer and lighter tones.

# Blue Tourmaline

ブルートルマリン

### 透明感あふれる深い青の魅力

深みのある青が多くの人を魅了するブルートルマリン。なかでも、藍染めの色に近いインディゴブルーのものは特別に「インディゴライトトルマリン」と呼ばれ、一段高い評価となります。稀少性が高く、10年前と比べても財産的価値が上昇し続けています。

また、アフガニスタンで採れたブルートルマリンが、パライバトルマリンに似ていると話題になったことがありました。ひときわ美しい青色が何よりの特徴で、ヨーロッパの色石市場ではコレクターズアイテムとなっています。

評価のポイントは色の濃さ。透明度が高く、深い青であるほど高く評価されます。深い青色を超えて黒ずんで見えると評価が下がります。

### The Allure of a Deep Blue Radiating Transparency

Blue tourmaline, renowned for its captivating deep blue colors, holds a special allure for many. Among these, stones with indigo tones are specifically referred to as "Indigolite Tourmaline," commanding particularly high value. Its rarity has driven a steady rise in investment value over the past decade.

At one point, blue tourmalines from Afghanistan gained attention for their resemblance to Paraiba tourmalines. With their strikingly vivid blue color, they have become prized collector's items in the European colored gemstone market.

The key factor in determining their value lies in the richness of their color. The more transparent and deeply blue the stone, the higher its valuation. However, if the color becomes overly dark and appears blackened, the value decreases.

(From top to bottom)
- YG Pendant_Blue Tourmaline1.95ct,D0.27ct
- Pt Ring_Indigolite Tourmaline4.67ct,D1.02ct
- Pt Ring_BlueTourmaline7.74ct,D1.1ct

## Color variations

藍に似た深い青が最も高い評価ですが、稀少性が高く幻となりつつあります。透明度とテリもチェックポイント。

A deep blue resembling indigo is the most highly valued, but its rarity is making it increasingly elusive. Transparency and luster are also key factors to consider.

# Green Tourmaline

グリーントルマリン

## エメラルドと見紛う美しい緑色

　深く美しい緑色が目を引くグリーントルマリン。その色ゆえに、長い間、エメラルドと混同されてきた歴史があります。

　グリーントルマリンについては、現在も市場に大きな石が出回っており、ブルートルマリンと比べると低価格での入手が可能です。ブラジル、スリランカなどで豊富に産出されるほか、アフリカのナイジェリア産の質が高く評価されています。

　色相は幅広く、深いエメラルドグリーンから青みの強いピーコックグリーン、やや黄みが入った若草色のものまであります。

　評価の基準は、深い色と透明度の高さ。ただ、近年は明るい緑の色合いのグリーントルマリンの人気が上昇し、販売価格も上がっています。

## A Beautiful Green Gem Mistaken for Emerald

Green tourmaline, with its deep and captivating green color, often catches the eye. Due to its color, it has long been mistaken for emeralds throughout history.

　Even today, large green tourmaline stones are readily available in the market and are more affordable than blue tourmalines. They are abundantly mined in regions like Brazil and Sri Lanka, with Nigerian green tourmalines from Africa being especially esteemed for their quality.

　The color range is remarkably diverse, spanning from deep emerald green to peacock green with strong blue tones, as well as bright, slightly yellowish greens reminiscent of fresh spring grass.

　The primary criteria for evaluating green tourmalines are their deep coloration and high transparency. However, in recent years, lighter green shades have risen in popularity, driving up their market prices.

(From top to bottom)
- Pt Ring_Green Tourmaline2.97ct,D0.658ct
- Green Tourmaline7.166ct
- Green Tourmaline4.49ct

## Color variations

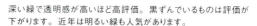

深い緑で透明感が高いほど高評価。黒ずんでいるものは評価が下がります。近年は明るい緑も人気があります。

The deeper and more transparent the green, the higher the value. However, stones with a blackish tone tend to be less desirable. In recent years, lighter shades of green have also gained popularity.

Tourmaline

### 優雅な濃い赤と可憐なピンク

赤いトルマリンはルベライトと呼ばれ、ルビーの代用石として利用された歴史があります。ラテン語で「赤」を意味する語に由来し、ルベライトと呼ばれるようになりました。ルビーに比べるとやや紫がかった赤色であり、ルビーより安価で市場には大粒の石も出回っています。評価のポイントは、赤い色の濃さと透明度の高さです。

一方、ピンクトルマリンはルベライトより淡い色。可憐で優しい雰囲気のパステルピンクから、やや紫がかったピンク、赤みが強いもの、ブラウンが入ったものなどもあります。価格も比較的手に入れやすい宝石です。

### Elegant Deep Red and Sweet Pink

The red tourmaline, also known as rubellite, has historically been used as a substitute for rubies. Its name derives from the Latin word for "red." Compared to rubies, rubellites display a slightly purplish-red color and are more affordable, with larger stones often available on the market. The key factors in determining their value are the depth of the red color and the level of transparency.

In contrast, pink tourmalines exhibit lighter shades than rubellites. Their colors range from soft, delicate pastel pinks to slightly purplish pinks, reddish tones, and even pinks with hints of brown. It is a gemstone that remains relatively accessible in terms of price.

# Rubellite & Pink Tourmaline

ルベライト & ピンクトルマリン

## Color variations

Rubellite

Pink Tourmaline

ルベライトは赤が濃く、透明感があるほど高い評価。黒ずんだものは評価が下がります。ピンクトルマリンはブラウンがかるとやや濁った印象を与え、評価が大きく下がります。

Rubellites are more highly valued when they display a deep red color and strong transparency. However, stones with a blackish tone are considered less desirable.
For pink tourmalines, a brownish tint can give the stone a slightly dull appearance, significantly reducing its value.

*(From top to bottom)*
・*Rubellite4.34ct*
・*Pt Pendant_Rubellite2.50ct,D0.05ct*
・*WG Pendant_Rubellite2.57ct,D0.06ct*
・*Pink Tourmaline3.01ct*

*(From the left to right)*
- Pt Pendant_Canary Tourmaline1.84ct,D0.102ct
- Canary Tourmaline2.08ct
- Canary Tourmaline4.70ct

# Yellow Tourmaline

イエロートルマリン

## Color variations

カナリー色が最高評価。透明度が高く、輝きが強いほど評価されます。黒味を帯びて感じるものは評価が下がります。

Canary yellow is the highest-rated. Stones with higher transparency and stronger brilliance receive higher evaluations, while those with a blackish color are rated lower.

## 明るいカナリー色が最高評価

　ブラジル、アフリカの鉱山では、同じ場所から各色のトルマリンが産出されます。そのなかでブラウンに次いで多く採れるのがイエロートルマリンです。絶対量が多いため入手しやすい価格であり、大変美しい石もあります。特に美しく、ファンが多いのがカナリー色のものです。

　色相はカナリー色から緑がかった草色系の黄色、ブラウンがかった黄色まであります。最も評価が高いのは、やはりカナリー色です。評価する際のポイントとしては、色の美しさに加え、輝きが強いものが高評価となります。

　黄色は金運を高める色であることから、インドなどでは人気が高い宝石です。

## Bright Canary Yellow Receives the Highest Rating

In the mines of Brazil and Africa, tourmalines of various colors are mined from the same locations. Among them, yellow tourmaline is the second most commonly found after brown. Its abundance makes it more affordable, yet some stones exhibit exceptional beauty. The canary-colored stones, in particular, are highly prized and have many admirers.

　The colors range from canary yellow to yellow-green tones with a grassy tint, and to yellow with brownish undertones. Among these, canary yellow remains the most highly valued. In evaluating these gemstones, the beauty of the color is crucial, and those with strong brilliance receive higher ratings.

　Yellow is associated with enhancing financial fortune, making it a popular gemstone in regions like India.

# Bicolor Tourmaline

バイカラートルマリン

## 魔法のように2色に分かれたトルマリン

ひとつの石が2色に分かれているバイカラートルマリン。結晶の成長過程で環境が激変して生まれると考えられ、稀少価値があります。ブラジル産は強い赤と緑がはっきりと分かれ、アフリカ産は2色に茶系の色みが加わっているのが特徴です。

スイカのように中心部の石を別の色の石が囲んでいるものはウォーターメロンと呼ばれ、きわめて稀少です。パライバトルマリンのウォーターメロンなど、美しい色の組み合わせであれば価格も評価も高まります。

評価のポイントは、2色がバランスよく、きれいに分かれていること。色の割合が1対1であることは稀で、さらに評価が高くなります。

## A Tourmaline Split Into Two Colors Like Magic

A single stone with two distinct colors is called a bicolor tourmaline. These stones are believed to form when the environment undergoes drastic changes during the crystal growth process, making them highly rare. Brazilian bicolor tourmalines are known for their sharp contrast between vivid red and green, while African varieties often feature brownish tones alongside the two colors.

Stones with a center encircled by a differently colored zone, resembling a watermelon, are called "watermelon tourmalines" and are exceptionally rare. When the color combination is particularly striking, such as in watermelon tourmalines from the Paraiba variety, both their value and evaluation increase significantly.

The primary evaluation criteria are that the two colors are well-balanced and distinctly separated. A perfectly even 1:1 color ratio is especially rare and commands a higher valuation.

(From the left to right)
- Bicolor Tourmaline1.77ct
- Bicolor Tourmaline19.54ct
- Watermelon Tourmaline5.03ct
- WG Pendant_Bicolor Paraiba Tourmaline3.0ct,D0.10ct
- Bicolor Tourmaline24.08ct

# Tourmaline Cat's Eye

トルマリンキャッツアイ

### 自然が生んだ猫目の美しさ

さまざまな色のトルマリンのなかには、カボションに研磨すると一条の線が浮かび上がる猫目効果があらわれる石があります。これらを総称してトルマリンキャッツアイといいます。自然が生み出す驚異の現象は稀有なものであり、同じトルマリンでも評価が上がる要素になります。

トルマリンキャッツアイのなかには、2色に分かれた境界線に一条の光の帯があらわれるバイカラートルマリンキャッツアイもあります。線が石の中央にはっきりと浮かび、コントラストが鮮明なものほど評価が高くなります。

ただ、色石なので色が美しいことが第一の評価ポイント。加えて、線がくっきりと浮かび、石の中央にあるものほど高評価となります。

### The Natural Beauty of Cat's Eyes

Among the various colors of tourmaline, some stones polished into a cabochon display a single line of light known as the "cat's eye effect." These are collectively referred to as tourmaline cat's eyes. This rare and extraordinary natural phenomenon adds significant value to tourmalines.

Within the category of tourmaline cat's eyes, there are also bicolor varieties where a line of light appears along the boundary between two colors. Stones with a well-defined line clearly visible in the center and a sharp color contrast are more highly valued.

However, as with all colored gemstones, the beauty of the color remains the primary evaluation criterion. In addition, stones with a sharp, distinct line that is centrally positioned receive the highest ratings.

(From top left to bottom)
- Tourmaline Cat's Eye 50.03ct
- Pt Ring_Tourmaline Cat's Eye 5.26ct, D0.20ct
- Rubellite Cat's Eye 24.08ct
- Bicolor Tourmaline Cat's Eye 9.50ct

# Tourmaline
## Production Trends and Value
トルマリンの産出動向とその価値

トルマリンは色の違いや稀少性により、財産的価値が5つにランク分けされます（次ページのランク表参照）。

トップに君臨するのがパライバトルマリン。1989年にブラジルのパライバ州バターリャで発見され、世界中で大人気となり品薄になるなか、1年で産出が止まってしまいました。隣りのリオグランデドノルテ州パレーリャスで鉱脈が見つかり、高品質で歓迎されましたが、今は採掘されていません。バターリャの周辺鉱山で青が薄くテリも強くない石がわずかに採れます。

その後、アフリカのナイジェリアで採掘が始まりました。ブラジル産に比べ薄い青色で、こちら

Tourmaline is classified into five ranks of financial value based on differences in color and rarity (refer to the ranking chart on the next page).

At the top of the ranks is Paraiba tourmaline. Discovered in 1989 in São José da Batalha, Paraíba State, Brazil, it quickly gained immense global popularity, leading to a significant supply shortage. Production ceased within a year. Later, a vein was discovered in Parelhas, Rio Grande do Norte State, yielding high-quality stones, but mining in this area has also stopped. Today, only a small number of stones with pale blue colors and weaker luster are being extracted from nearby mines around Batalha.

Mining subsequently began in Nigeria, Africa. Nigerian stones have a lighter blue color compared to Brazilian ones, but mining stopped there as well in 2005. The next major discovery was in Mozambique. Mozambican tourmalines are often highly transparent but tend to have pale colors, with very

グリーントルマリン　Green Tourmaline

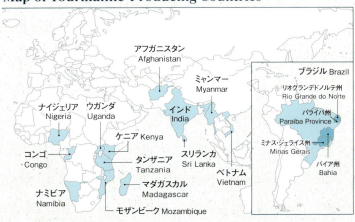

**Map of Tourmaline-Producing Countries**

※おもな産出国や地域を記載しています
※Main producing countries and regions

# Tourmaline
## Production Trends and Value
トルマリンの産出動向とその価値

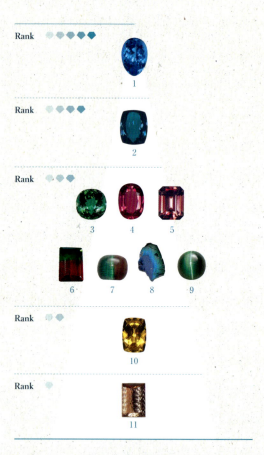

### Rank by Type

**1 Paraiba Tourmaline**
Brazil／Mozambique／Nigeria

**2 Blue Tourmaline**
Brazil／Nigeria／Namibia／
Kenya／Madagascar／
Afghanistan

**3 Green Tourmaline**
Brazil／Kenya／Tanzania／
Nigeria／Afghanistan／
Uganda／Congo／
Madagascar／Sri Lanka

**4 Rubellite**
Brazil／Tanzania／Namibia／
Myanmar／Afghanistan／
Kenya／Madagascar／
Sri Lanka／Vietnam／India

**5 Pink Tourmaline**
Brazil／Namibia／Tanzania／
Vietnam／Kenya／Madagascar／
Afghanistan／India

**6 Bicolor Tourmaline**
Brazil／Tanzania／
Namibia／Kenya／Madagascar

**7 Bicolor Tourmaline Cat's Eye**
Brazil

**8 Watermelon Tourmaline**
Brazil

**9 Tourmaline Cat's Eye**
Brazil

**10 Yellow Tourmaline**
Tanzania／Kenya／Brazil／
Madagascar

**11 Brown Tourmaline**
Brazil／Tanzania／Kenya／
Namibia

---

も2005年には採れなくなりました。次に発見されたのはモザンビーク。モザンビーク産は透明度が高くて色が薄いものが多く、ブラジル産のネオンブルーのようなものはわずかです。モザンビークでもすでに鉱脈は枯れています。

このように、パライバトルマリンの産出は減る一方です。しかし、人気は突出して高く、今後も価格は上昇し続けると考えられ、投資目的の購入が多く見られます。

そもそもトルマリンには、全般的にブラジル、アフリカ、中東のアフガニスタン、アジアなど幅広い産地があります。ひとつの鉱山から種類の違ういくつものトルマリンが採れることもあります。産出地によって、驚くほど特徴と評価が異なる場合もあることは覚えておきましょう。

さて、2番目に高いランクにあるのは、ブルートルマリン。ブラジル、ナミビア、ナイジェリア

few resembling the vivid neon blue of Brazilian stones. Mining in Mozambique has also exhausted the veins.

Thus, the production of Paraiba tourmaline continues to decline. However, its popularity remains extremely high, and prices are expected to continue rising, leading to many purchases for investment purposes.

In general, tourmaline has a wide range of origins, including Brazil, Africa, the Middle East (Afghanistan), and Asia. A single mine can produce several different types of tourmaline. Keep in mind that characteristics and evaluations can vary significantly depending on the origin.

The second-highest rank is blue tourmaline, which is mined in Brazil, Namibia, and Nigeria. Brazilian blue-green stones are particularly popular, while Nigerian stones are scarce and rarely appear on the market.

The third rank is green tourmaline, rubellite, and pink tourmaline. Green tourmaline is mined in Brazil, Africa, Sri Lanka, Afghanistan, and other locations, and its prices are stable. Nigerian stones are of good quality and highly regarded. Rubellite

などで産出され、ブラジル産のブルーグリーンの石が特に人気です。ナイジェリア産は量が少なく、あまり市場に出ることがありません。

3番目のランクは、グリーントルマリン、ルベライト、ピンクトルマリンなど。グリーントルマリンはブラジル、アフリカ、スリランカ、アフガニスタンなどで産出され、価格も安定しています。ナイジェリア産の石は良質で高く評価されます。ルベライトとピンクトルマリンの産地は、主にブラジルとアフガニスタン。一般的にブラジル産のほうが質が良いといわれます。

バイカラートルマリン、バイカラートルマリンキャッツアイ、ウォーターメロントルマリン、トルマリンキャッツアイなどのユニークなトルマリンについては、色と品質によっては1ランク上に評価されることもあります。

バイカラートルマリンの産地は、ブラジル以外ではナイジェリア、マダガスカルなどで少量の産出があるのみ。近年は、ブラジル産の採掘量も減り、稀少価値がさらに高まっています。

4番目のランクのイエロートルマリン、5番目のブラウントルマリンは産出量が多く、トルマリンのなかでは手軽に購入できます。

いずれも購入を検討する際は、色、内包物、輝きがチェックポイント（p.160参照）。色は深く濃いほうが高評価となります。内包物は少ないほうがよいですが、天然の色石の証でもあり、美しさを損なっていなければ神経質になる必要もありません。透明度が高く、輝きの強い石を選びましょう。

and pink tourmaline are mainly sourced from Brazil and Afghanistan, with Brazilian stones generally considered to be of higher quality.

Unique tourmalines, such as bicolor tourmaline, bicolor tourmaline cat's eye, watermelon tourmaline, and tourmaline cat's eye, may sometimes be rated one rank higher depending on their color and quality.

Bicolor tourmaline is mined in small quantities outside Brazil, such as in Nigeria and Madagascar. In recent years, Brazilian production has also decreased, further increasing its rarity.

The fourth rank is yellow tourmaline, and the fifth rank is brown tourmaline. These stones are abundant and are relatively affordable within the tourmaline category.

When considering a purchase, focus on the color, inclusions, and brilliance (see p.160). Deeper and richer colors are more highly valued. Fewer inclusions are better, but as they are a natural feature of colored stones, it's unnecessary to be overly concerned as long as they do not detract from the beauty. Opt for stones with high transparency and strong brilliance.

パライバトルマリン　Paraiba Tourmaline

(Top)
- Pt Pendant_Rhodolite Garnet3.91ct,Hauynite0.15ct,D0.53ct

(Middle row left to right)
- Pt Ring_Dragon Garnet3.62ct,D0.037ct
- WG Ring_Green Garnet2.70ct,D0.217ct
- Pt Ring_Demantoid Garnet1.30ct,D0.30ct
- WG Pendant_Spessartite Garnet11.41ct,D0.40ct
- YG Ring_Malaya Garnet1.96ct,D0.33ct

(Bottom left to right)
- Mandarin Garnet2.53ct
- Color-change Garnet3.79ct
- Mali Garnet4.52ct

# Garnet

ガーネット

## 深紅から緑まで多彩な色相の魅力

　ガーネットは赤い石と考えられがちですが、深紅から赤茶、紫、緑、オレンジまで豊かな色相があります。これはガーネットが単一の石ではなく、同じ結晶構造を持つ石の総称であるため。鉱物に入り込んだ金属元素の組み合わせにより、色合いのみならず硬度にも違いがあります。厳密に分類すると、14〜20種類にもなるといわれます。

　暗闇を進むノアの箱舟を赤い輝きで照らしたと神話に描かれる一方、21世紀になって発見された新種もあり、歴史もそれぞれ異なります。

## The Allure of Colors from Deep Scarlet to Green

Garnets are often considered red stones, but they exhibit a wide range of colors, including deep scarlet, reddish-brown, purple, green, and orange. This diversity arises because garnet is not a single gemstone but a group of stones sharing the same crystal structure. Variations in color and hardness are determined by the combination of metallic elements within the mineral. When classified precisely, garnets are said to include 14 to 20 different types.

Mythology describes garnets as emitting a red glow to guide Noah's Ark through the darkness, yet new varieties have continued to be discovered even in the 21st century, each with its own distinct history.

# Demantoid
# Garnet

デマントイドガーネット

### Color variations

Russian

Namibia, Africa

ロシア産はテリのある緑色が特徴で、色が濃く透明度が高いものが高評価。ナミビア産はロシア産に比べ色が薄い傾向です。

Russian demantoids are known for their vivid green brilliance, with richly colored and highly transparent stones being the most highly valued. In contrast, Namibian demantoids tend to have a paler color compared to their Russian counterparts.

*(From top to bottom)*
- Pt Ring_Demantoid Garnet0.85ct
- Pt Ring_Demantoid Garnet1.11ct,D2.90ct
- WG Pendant_Demantoid Garnet2.40ct
- Pt Pendant_Demantoid Garnet1.09ct,D0.20ct

## ロマノフ朝の宮廷で光り輝いた石

　黄緑から緑色の煌めきがダイヤモンドのように眩いデマントイドガーネット。デマントイドという名称自体が、オランダ語で「ダイヤモンドに似た」という意味です。

　1853年頃、ロシアのウラル山脈で発見。当時の統治者ロマノフ朝の王侯貴族はたちまち魅了され、王室御用達の伝説の宝石細工師ファベルジェもこの石を使いました。ロシアでは20世紀に入ると産出されなくなり、稀少性が非常に高くなっています。アフリカのナミビア、パキスタンなどでも採れますが、全体的に色合いが薄く、価格にも大きな違いがあります。内包物が馬のしっぽのように針状に入っている石は「ホーステール」といわれ、逆に珍重されます。1カラットを超える大粒のものは非常に少なく市場に出回るのは稀です。

## A Gemstone That Shone Brightly in the Romanov Court

Demantoid garnet shines with dazzling brilliance in yellow-green to green colors, resembling a diamond. The name "demantoid" comes from the Dutch word meaning "diamond-like."

　Discovered around 1853 in Russia's Ural Mountains, it quickly captivated the aristocracy of the Romanov dynasty. Even Fabergé, the renowned jeweler to the royal family, used it in his creations. By the 20th century, production in Russia had ceased, making these gems exceptionally rare.

　Demantoid garnets are also found in Namibia and Pakistan, but these stones often have paler colors and lower value. Uniquely, stones with needle-like inclusions resembling a horse's tail, known as "horsetails," are considered highly desirable. Stones over 1 carat are extremely rare and seldom seen on the market.

(From top to bottom)
- YG Pendant_Green Garnet2.08ct,D0.181ct
- Pt Ring_Green Garnet1.39ct,D0.63ct
- YG Ring_Green Garnet1.56ct,D0.445ct
- Pt Ring_Green Garnet1.105ct,D1.31ct
- Pt Ring_Green Garnet1.56ct,D0.61ct

# Green Garnet

グリーンガーネット

### 採掘地により別名をもつ深い緑の石

　落ち着いた緑の色合いが、日本市場で大変人気の高いグリーンガーネット。良質なものはエメラルドに匹敵するほど高く評価されます。エメラルドに内包物が多い特徴があるのに対し、グリーンガーネットは内包物が少なく、透明度が高い深い緑色であることが人気に拍車をかけました。
　アメリカのティファニー社は、ケニアのツァボで採れた深い緑で透明度の高いグリーンガーネットを「ツァボライト」と名付けて、売り出しました。同じアフリカのタンザニアも主要産出国であり、色の濃い石もありますが、全般的に色が薄い傾向があります。残念なことに両国とも高品質な石の産出が見られなくなって産出量も減り、10数年で価格が約10倍にも上昇しています。

### A Deep Green Stone with Different Names Depending on Its Mining Location

Green garnet, with its calm green tone, is highly popular in the Japanese market. High-quality stones are highly valued, rivaling emeralds in price. Unlike emeralds, which are known for their numerous inclusions, green garnets have fewer inclusions, a deep green color, and high transparency, further enhancing their appeal.

　Tiffany & Co. named the deep green, transparent green garnets mined in Kenya's Tsavo region "Tsavorite" and introduced them to the market. Tanzania, another major producer in Africa, also produces richly colored stones, though they are generally lighter in tone. Unfortunately, both countries have experienced a decline in the production of high-quality stones, and their overall output has decreased. Over the past decade, prices have risen approximately tenfold.

## Color variations

エメラルドカットは特に透明度が重要。オーバル、ハートシェイプはカットが生み出すグリーンの濃淡のモザイク模様が魅力。

For emerald cuts, transparency is especially important. Oval and heart shapes are valued for the mosaic-like green patterns created by the cut.

Garnet

# Color-change Garnet

カラーチェンジガーネット

## 光源により色が変わる不思議

　カラーチェンジガーネットは文字通り、色が変わるガーネット。自然光のもとでは青や緑に輝く石が、白熱灯に照らされると赤や茶色、紫色に変わります。魔法のような変化が起こる理由は、含有されるバナジウムに加え、他の元素が内部に入り込んでいるためだと考えられています。

　発見されたのは1970年代と歴史は浅く、日本で流通し始めたのはほんの十数年前のことです。

　アレキサンドライトのように美しく赤紫から青緑へ変化するカラーチェンジガーネットが、最高の評価を受けて人気を博しました。ただし、すでに産出がとまり、ほとんど流通していません。茶色から緑に変わる石はケニア、タンザニア、マダガスカルなどで採掘が続いています。

## The Mystery of Color Change Under Different Light Sources

Color-change garnet, as the name implies, is a garnet that changes color. Under natural light, it appears blue or green, but under incandescent light, it shifts to red, brown, or purple. This magical transformation is thought to result from vanadium combined with other elements within the stone.

　Discovered in the 1970s, its history is relatively short, and it began circulating in the Japanese market only about a decade ago.

　Garnets that change from reddish-purple to blue-green, similar to alexandrite, have received the highest acclaim and gained great popularity. However, production of these gems has ceased, and they are rarely seen on the market. Stones that shift from brown to green are still mined in Kenya, Tanzania, and Madagascar.

**Incandescent light**　　**Natural light**

 白熱灯　　 自然光

## Color variations

白熱灯と自然光では色が変わります。色の変化が大きいほど価値は高まり、どんな色みに変化するかも重要ポイントです。

The color shifts between incandescent light and natural light. The greater the change, the higher the value, with the specific colors it transitions to being key evaluation points.

*(Clockwise from top left)*
- *YG Pendant_Color-change Garnet1.29ct,D0.07ct*
- *YG Pendant_Color-change Garnet2.24ct,D0.26ct*
- *Color-change Garnet3.27ct*
- *Color-change Garnet2.15ct*

# Rhodolite Garnet

ロードライトガーネット

## バラの花のような紫がかった赤い石

バラの花を思わせる紫がかった赤色が美しいロードライトガーネット。その名称自体が、ギリシャ語で「バラの花のような石」という意味合いの言葉に由来します。

発見されたのは19世紀の終わり頃で、比較的新しい種類のガーネットです。主な産地は、タンザニア、マダガスカル、スリランカなど。産出量が安定しているため比較的手頃な価格で流通していましたが、徐々に値上がりしてきています。エレガントな色で大粒の石も採れるのも人気の理由。

近年では、モザンビークの鉱山で2009年頃から採掘されるようになった、ぶどうのような紫色のロードライトガーネットが「グレープガーネット」と名付けられ、注目されるようになりました。

(From top to bottom)
- WG Ring_Rhodolite Garnet6.26ct, Hauynite0.11ct,D0.05ct
- YG Ring_Rhodolite Garnet5.27ct,D0.22ct
- WG Ring_Rhodolite Garnet7.96ct,D1.01ct
- WG Ring_Rhodolite Garnet4.43ct,D0.27ct
- WG Pendant_Rhodolite Garnet8.49ct,D0.06ct

## A Purplish-Red Stone Resembling a Rose

Rhodolite garnet, with its purplish-red color reminiscent of a rose, derives its name from the Greek word meaning "stone like a rose flower."

Discovered in the late 19th century, it is a relatively new variety of garnet. Major sources include Tanzania, Madagascar, and Sri Lanka. Stable production once kept prices affordable, but they have been gradually increasing. Its elegant color and the availability of large stones add to its appeal.

In recent years, a grape-like purple rhodolite garnet mined in Mozambique since around 2009, referred to as "grape garnet," has gained notable attention.

## Color variations

赤い色が濃いほど高評価。ただし、黒ずんだ印象を与えるものは評価が下がります。内包物が少なく、透明度が高いかをチェック。

The deeper the red, the higher the value. However, stones with a dark or blackish appearance are rated lower. Look for minimal inclusions and high transparency.

Garnet

## 褐色みを帯びた赤からオレンジ系まで

スペッサータイトガーネットは、ドイツのスペッサルト地方にちなんで名付けられた赤いガーネットです。ひと言で赤といっても、褐色を帯びた赤色からオレンジ系まで色みの幅が広いことが特徴です。産地の地質の違いによって違いが生まれるといわれています。

スペッサータイトガーネットのなかでも、明るく鮮やかなオレンジ色に輝くものはフルーツのマンダリンの色を思い起こさせ、「マンダリンガーネット」と呼ばれます。中国で特に人気が高く、市場価値が上がっています。

スペッサータイトガーネットも、10数年前までは手頃な価格で入手可能でしたが、産出が減っており、価格が上昇しています。

## From Brownish-Red to Orange

Spessartite garnet is a red garnet named after the *Spessart* region in Germany. Its color ranges widely, from brownish-red to orange, with variations attributed to the geological differences of its mining locations.

Bright and vivid orange spessartite garnets, reminiscent of mandarin fruit, are called "mandarin garnets." They are especially popular in China, leading to an increase in their market value.

About a decade ago, spessartite garnets were relatively affordable, but production has declined, causing their prices to rise.

# Mandarin Garnet & Spessartite Garnet

マンダリンガーネット & スペッサータイトガーネット

### Color variations

Spessartite Garnet

赤からオレンジ系まで幅広い色相。色の濃さと透明感、眩い輝きを重視しましょう。カットやキズの有無にも注意。

A wide range of colors from red to orange. Focus on color depth, transparency, and dazzling brilliance. Pay attention to the cut and the presence of any blemishes.

(*Clockwise from top left*)
- YG Pendant_Spessartite Garnet0.915ct,D0.01ct
- YG Earrings_Spessartite Garnet0.91ct,0.90ct,D0.15ct
- Pt Pendant_Spessartite Garnet4.29ct,D0.45ct
- *Mandarin Garnet5.693ct*

*(From left to right)*
- *Mali Garnet 2.75ct*
- *Mali Garnet 2.61ct*
- *Mali Garnet 7.58ct*
- *Mali Garnet 1.14ct*

# Mali Garnet

マリガーネット

## 稀少なクロムグリーンが最高評価

20世紀の終わりにガーネットの仲間に加わったマリガーネット。1994年に西アフリカのマリで発見され、翌年には大量に採掘されて注目を集めました。ただし、現在、市場に出回っているのは世紀が変わる頃までに採れたものがほとんど。以降はわずかしか産出されていません。

グロッシュラーとアンドラダイトの2種のガーネットが混合してできた石で、アンドラダイトの特性である屈折率の高さと鮮やかな輝きを有しています。色は黄色から緑、茶色など多彩。最も高く評価されるのは稀少なクロムグリーンですが、輝きの強いものはいずれも美しく人気があります。

## The Rare Chrome Green Receives the Highest Evaluation

Mali garnet joined the garnet family at the end of the 20th century, following its discovery in 1994 in Mali, West Africa. It gained attention the following year with large-scale mining. However, most Mali garnet on the market today was mined by the turn of the century, with very limited production since then.

This gemstone is a combination of grossular and andradite garnets, inheriting the high refractive index and vivid brilliance of andradite. Its colors range from yellow to green and brown. The rare chrome green variety is the most highly valued, though all brilliantly luminous stones are admired and popular.

# Malaya Garnet

マラヤガーネット

### Color variations

マダガスカル産は紫系、タンザニアのウンバ鉱山で採れるのはやや茶色系、赤みが強いのはケニア産。

Garnets from Madagascar are purplish, those from Tanzania's Umba mines are slightly brownish, and Kenya produces ones with strong reddish tones

## 20世紀後半に発見されたガーネット

マラヤガーネットは、スペッサータイトガーネットとパイロープガーネットという種類が混合してできたガーネットです。スペッサータイトガーネットに含まれるマンガンとアルミニウムから生まれる色はオレンジ系、パイロープガーネットのマグネシウムとアルミニウムから生まれるのは赤い色み。両者が混ざり合ったマラヤガーネットでは、オレンジやピンク、茶色を帯びた赤など特別な色相となり、独特な魅力を放ちます。

発見されたのは1979年と歴史が浅く、当初はスペッサータイトと混同されていました。鉱物学的な違いがわかり、稀少価値が認められ人気となっています。

ケニアで採掘される赤みが強いマラヤガーネットは非常にレアで、特に注目されています。

## Garnet Discovered in the Late 20th Century

Malaya garnet is a type of garnet formed by a combination of spessartite and pyrope garnets. The manganese and aluminum in spessartite produce orange colors, while the magnesium and aluminum in pyrope create red tones. These elements combine in Malaya garnet to produce unique shades such as orange, pink, and reddish-brown, giving the gemstone its distinctive allure.

Discovered in 1979, it has a relatively short history and was initially mistaken for spessartite. Once its mineralogical differences were identified, its rarity and value gained recognition, boosting its popularity.

Malaya garnet with strong reddish tones, particularly those mined in Kenya, is highly rare and especially prized.

*(Clockwise from top left)*
- *YG Pendant_Malaya Garnet1.52ct,D0.105ct*
- *WG Pendant_Malaya Garnet2.25ct,D0.04ct,0.014ct*
- *Malaya Garnet3.11ct*

(From top to bottom)
- Pt Pendant_Dragon Garnet3.62ct,D0.21ct
- Pt Ring_Dragon Garnet1.08ct,Green Diamond 0.156ct,Gray Diamond0.22ct,Pallasite Peridot0.05ct
- Pt／YG Ring_Dragon Garnet9.58ct,D0.17ct
- YG Pendant_Dragon Garnet13.72ct
- Dragon Garnet15.60ct

# Dragon Garnet

ドラゴンガーネット

*(From top left to right)*
- YG Ring_Dragon Garnet1.00ct,D0.16ct
- Pt Ring_Dragon Garnet1.21ct,D0.45ct
- Pt/YG Pendant_Dragon Garnet2.17ct,Green Diamond0.184ct,D0.08ct
- WG Pendant_Dragon Garnet1.06ct,D0.09ct

## 龍の名にふさわしい赤い蛍光

　ドラゴンガーネットは、2022年にタンザニアで発見され、2023年に世界最大のミネラルショー・ツーソンジェムショーでお披露目されると、瞬く間に人気となりました。パイロープ、アルマンダイト、スペッサータイトの3種類のガーネットが混ざったとても珍しい石です。クロムとバナジウムを含有しており、多くのものはUVライトを当てると赤い蛍光色を発色しますが、中には色が変化しないものもあります。

　ドラゴンという名前は、変色した時の赤い蛍光色が、まるで龍の眼の色のように見えることから名付けられました。色相は、赤褐色の濃い色みから、パパラチアサファイアのような淡いピンクオレンジ、淡いピンク紫など幅広くあります。パパラチアに似た色合いのものは稀少で、海外でも人気が高くなっています。タンザニアでの発見後、タンザニアとケニアの国境付近からも産出していますが、量が少ない上、急激に世界的な人気が高まったため、すでに値上がりしています。赤く鮮やかに蛍光する石は少なく、稀少価値は高くなっています。

### Changes under UV light

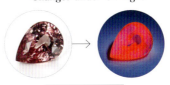

UVライトをあてると蛍光する石もあります
Some exhibit fluorescence

## Red Fluorescence Befitting a Dragon

Dragon garnet was discovered in Tanzania in 2022 and made its debut at the 2023 Tucson Gem Show, the world's largest mineral showcase, where it quickly gained widespread popularity. This exceptionally rare gemstone is a unique blend of three garnet varieties: pyrope, almandine, and spessartite. It contains chromium and vanadium, and most specimens fluoresce a vivid red under UV light, although some do not exhibit this property.

The name "Dragon Garnet" was inspired by the red fluorescence that appears during color changes, resembling the fiery eyes of a dragon. The gemstone's colors range from deep reddish-brown to soft pink-orange and light pink-purple, reminiscent of padparadscha sapphire. Specimens with padparadscha-like tones are particularly rare and have garnered significant international interest. Following its initial discovery in Tanzania, additional deposits have been found near the Tanzania-Kenya border. However, production remains limited, and the gem's soaring global popularity has already driven up prices. Brightly fluorescent red specimens are especially scarce, further enhancing their value and rarity.

# Garnet
## Production Trends and Value
ガーネットの産出動向とその価値

**Rank by Type**

❶ **Demantoid Garnet**
Russia／Iran／
Namibia／Pakistan
＊5 stars only for Russian products

❷ **Green Garnet**
Kenya／Tanzania

❸ **Color-Change Garnet**
Tanzania／Madagascar／
Kenya

❹ **Spessartite Garnet**
Tanzania／Sri Lanka／
Madagascar

❺ **Rhodolite Garnet**
Sri Lanka／Tanzania／
Madagascar／Mozambique／Brazil

❻ **Mandarin Garnet**
Tanzania／Sri Lanka／
Madagascar

❼ **Malaya Garnet**
Kenya／Tanzania／Madagascar

❽ **Mali Garnet**
Kenya／Tanzania／Madagascar

❾ **Dragon Garnet**
Kenya／Tanzania／Madagascar

❿ **Almandite Garnet**
Brazil／Tanzania／Madagascar／
Mozambique

ガーネットは多種類の石の総称であるため、それぞれ評価は大きく異なります。最高ランクのデマントイドガーネットの一級品と一番下のアルマンダイトガーネットでは、1カラットあたりの価格が50倍、時には100倍ほども違います。

デマントイドガーネットは、19世紀半ばにロシアのウラル山脈で発見され、20世紀に入ると産出が減って幻の宝石といわれるようになりました。2002年に再び採掘が始まったものの、採れたのは8.5キロの原石のみで半年で閉山。宝石品質の良質な原石はわずか600グラムだったといわれます。0.1カラットの小粒でも非常に高価です。

二番目のグリーンガーネットの主要産地はケニアとタンザニア。ケニアのツァボ国立公園一帯

Since garnet is a collective term for various types of stones, their valuations differ significantly. For instance, the price per carat of top-quality demantoid garnet can be 50 times, or even 100 times, higher than that of the lowest-ranked almandite garnet.

Demantoid garnet was discovered in the mid-19th century in Russia's Ural Mountains. By the 20th century, its production declined, earning it the reputation of a "phantom gem." While mining resumed in 2002, only 8.5 kilograms of rough stones were extracted within six months before the mine closed again. It is said that only 600 grams of gem-quality rough stones were recovered. Even small stones of 0.1 carats are extremely expensive.

The second-ranked green garnet primarily comes from Kenya and Tanzania. In Kenya, the Tsavo National Park region produces deep green

# Garnet

## Map of Garnet-Producing Countries

※おもな産出国や地域を記載しています
※Main producing countries and regions

では、透明度の高い深い緑の石が採れます。一方のタンザニア産は緑色が薄いものが主流。両国とも産出が減り、急激に値上りしています。カラーチェンジガーネットは、タンザニアのメレラニ鉱山の赤紫色から青緑色に変わる石が最高評価ですが、産出はストップ。ケニア、タンザニア（メレラニ鉱山以外）、マダガスカルでは茶色から緑色に変わる石が産出されます。

　三番目のランクのスペッサータイトガーネットは、スリランカでの産出が激減し、ほとんどがアフリカ産です。全体的に産出量が減り、価格が上昇しています。マンダリンガーネットの主要産地はタンザニアとマダガスカルです。

　ロードライトガーネットの主な産出国は、タンザニア、マダガスカル、スリランカなど。2009年頃からモザンビークの鉱山で色合いの美しい原石が産出されるようになりました。マリガーネットは、1990年代半ばにマリで豊富に産出されましたが、2000年に入ってからはストップしており、稀少性が高まっています。

　マラヤガーネットの主な産出国はケニアとタンザニア。ケニアのツァボ国立公園近くで非常にレアな赤い石が産出されますが、マサイ族の居住地域ゆえ採掘できず、稀少性が高くなっています。ドラゴンガーネットは、2022年に大きな鉱床が発見されて以来、現在は比較的安定した産出が見られています。

stones with high transparency, whereas Tanzanian stones tend to have lighter green colors. Production in both countries has decreased, leading to sharp price increases. The highest-rated color-change garnets, which shift from reddish-purple to blue-green and are mined in Tanzania's Merelani mines, are no longer being produced. However, stones that change from brown to green are still mined in Kenya, Tanzania(except for Merelani mines), and Madagascar.

Third-ranked spessartite garnet is now primarily sourced from Africa, as production in Sri Lanka has drastically decreased. Overall production is declining, leading to rising prices. Mandarin garnet's main sources are Tanzania and Madagascar.

Rhodolite garnet is primarily mined in Tanzania, Madagascar, and Sri Lanka. Since around 2009, Mozambique has also produced rough stones with beautiful colors. Mali garnet was abundantly mined in Mali in the mid-1990s but production has been halted since 2000, making it increasingly rare.

Malaya garnet is primarily sourced from Kenya and Tanzania. Rare red stones are found near Kenya's Tsavo National Park but cannot be mined due to the area being inhabited by the Maasai people, further increasing their rarity. Dragon garnet has seen relatively stable production since the discovery of a large deposit in 2022.

ケニア産
ツァボライトの原石
Rough Tsavorite
from Kenya

# マハラジャも庶民も親しんだ インドの宝石の歴史

## History of Gemstones in India: Loved by Both Maharajas and Commoners

私はインド北西部の宝石の街ジャイプールで、宝石商の父のもと、宝石に親しんで育ちました。インドでは歴史の中、そして現在の生活の中にも宝石が密接に関わっています。

インドの宝石と聞いて、まず皆さんが思い浮かべるのがマハラジャではないでしょうか。インド各藩の領主であったマハラジャは、富の象徴や装飾品として宝石を身に着けただけでなく、お守りとして邪気を遠ざけ、幸運を招くものとして、謁見の時には大きな宝石の付いた王冠を被りました。また、お城のシャンデリアを本物の宝石で作ったり、壁に宝石を埋め込んだりと、身に着ける以外にもさまざまなかたちで宝石を活用していました。

インドで宝石に親しんできたのはマハラジャ

I grew up in Jaipur, a gem city in northwest India, surrounded by gemstones under the guidance of my father, a gemstone merchant. In India, gemstones have been deeply intertwined with both history and daily life.

When you think of Indian gemstones, the first thing that likely comes to mind is the Maharajas. The Maharajas, rulers of various Indian states, not only adorned themselves with gemstones as symbols of wealth and decoration but also used them as talismans to ward off evil and bring good fortune. During audiences, they wore crowns adorned with large gemstones. Beyond personal adornment, they utilized gemstones in various ways, such as creating chandeliers out of real gemstones or embedding them into walls to protect and energize their homes and workplaces.

## Interview

インドの宝石商

### サンディープ・ラワット氏

**Indian Gem Dealer**
**Mr. Sandeep Rawat**

のような大金持ちだけではありません。インドでは体調が悪いとき、人生で何か上手くいかないことがある時、人々は寺院へ相談にいきます。そこでは、「この宝石を持つと改善しますよ」と教えてくれます。そして、それぞれの予算にあわせて宝石を購入し、それをもって善くなるようにと祈ります。

ナワラタナという9つの宝石があしらわれたジュエリーは、お守りとしてインドで人気があります。9つの宝石はエメラルド、ルビー、ブルーサファイア、珊瑚、真珠、ダイヤモンド、アクアマリン、クリソベリルキャッツアイ、イエローサファイアで、それぞれの宝石が別々の惑星とリンクして、異なるエネルギーを受け取ることができると信じられています。人はその日によって必要

「信頼」の大切さを教えてくれた父とともに
Together with my father, who taught me the value of trust

なエネルギーが違いますが、ナワラタナで9つの宝石を同時に身に着ければ、マルチビタミンのようにすべてに作用してくれるというわけです。

このようにインドの長い歴史のなかで宝石は、権力の象徴としてだけでなく、護符、お守りとして、王様から庶民まで、幅広い人々に愛されてきました。

However, it wasn't only the wealthy Maharajas who had close ties to gemstones. In India, when someone feels unwell or experiences challenges in life, they often seek advice at a temple. They are then told, "Carrying this gemstone will improve your situation." Based on their budget, they purchase a gemstone and pray for better circumstances while holding it.

Jewelry featuring nine gemstones, known as *Navaratna*, is popular as an amulet in India. The nine gemstones—emerald, ruby, blue sapphire, coral, pearl, diamond, aquamarine, chrysoberyl cat's eye, and yellow sapphire—are believed to be linked to different planets, each receiving distinct energies. Though a person may need different energies on different days, wearing the *Navaratna*, which combines all nine gemstones, is believed to act like a multivitamin, offering benefits for all aspects of life.

Thus, throughout India's long history, gemstones have been loved by a wide range of people, from royalty to commoners, not only as symbols of power but also as protective charms and talismans.

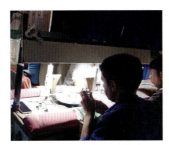

サンディープ氏の会社が運営する研磨工場の様子
At the cutting and polishing workshop operated by Mr. Sandeep's company

## Profile

ロイヤルカラー株式会社 代表取締役
ROYAL COLOR CO., LTD CEO

ナワラタナの9つの宝石。これらで指輪やペンダントを作ります
Nine gemstones of *Navaratna*, used for rings and pendants

047

ピンクの壁が美しいジャイプールの街並み
The picturesque streets of Jaipur with its beautiful pink walls

### 信頼が鍵となり発展した
### インドの宝石ビジネス

　そのなかで発展したのが、私の故郷であるラジャスタン州の州都ジャイプール。インド最大の宝石の集積地であり、研磨や加工も盛んです。国内やタイ、スリランカなど周辺国のみならず、アフリカの国々からも多くの原石が集まり、街の半分の人が宝石産業に従事していた時期もあったほどです。

　私が宝石商である父から学んだ宝石ビジネスの発展の鍵は「信頼」です。これは他の産業にもいえることですが、インドでは数十年前までビジネスの際に契約書にサインをすることは一般的ではありませんでした。取引する相手のことを信頼しているから、書面に残して互いに写しをもって

# 変わりゆく
# 世界の宝石市場

## The Changing
## Global Gemstone Market

### The Gemstone Business in India:
### Built on Trust

One of the places where this developed is Jaipur, the capital of Rajasthan, my hometown. Jaipur is India's largest hub for gemstones and is also renowned for its polishing and processing activities. Rough stones are gathered not only from within the country and neighboring nations like Thailand and Sri Lanka but also from African countries. At one point, half the city's population was engaged in the gemstone industry.

　The key to the development of the gemstone business, which I learned from my father, a gemstone merchant, is "trust." This can be said for other industries as well, but until a few decades ago in India, it was not common practice to sign contracts for business deals. This was because people trusted their business partners so deeply that there was no need to leave a written record or keep copies of agreements. Everyone knew that "trust takes 100 years to build and just one second to break," and they would never deceive someone they truly trusted.

　Today, influenced by Western practices, contracts, certificates, and other documentation have become important in Indian business as well. However, I believe that for industries dealing with high-value items like gemstones to continue to thrive, it is also important to maintain the broad-minded and human-centered relationships, based on "trust," that were characteristic of the old India.

　With the passage of time, the global gemstone market and its distribution have undergone significant changes. Like other industries, the movement of people and goods has become more dynamic, and

Interview **Mr.Sandeep Rawat**

おく必要がなかったのです。なぜなら、誰もが「信頼は築くのに100年かかり、1秒で壊れる」と知っており、心から信頼している相手を欺くことは決してなかったからです。

現在はインドのビジネスも欧米の影響を受け、契約書、鑑別書などの書面が重要になってきています。しかし、宝石のような高額なものを扱う産業が発展するためには、昔のインドのように「信頼」をベースとする、大らかで人間的な関係性もまた重要なのではないかと感じています。

時代の変遷とともに、世界の宝石市場や流通も様変わりしました。他の産業同様、人とモノの移動が盛んになり、すべてのスピードが速くなっています。かつてはインドから日本に商品を送るのに約1カ月かかりましたが、今は最短2日で届きます。

インターネットの普及は、宝石取引のありようを大きく変えました。以前はアフリカ奥地の鉱山で良い石が出たという噂を聞いても、簡単には足を運べず、真偽を確かめるのは困難でした。しかし、今はどんな山奥の秘境からでも、宝石の画像や動画を受け取り、世界のどこにいても瞬時に確認することができます。

国や地域による好みの違いは、インターネット時代になって薄れてきています。例えば、中国ではかつてヒスイを中心に十大宝石に人気が集中していましたが、最近はガーネットやトルマリンなどの認知度も高まっています。

これからの色石選びの最大のポイントは、やはり稀少性だと思います。なかでも産出がストップし、市場に出回っている石しかない状態なら、今後確実に値上がりします。たとえばパライバトルマリンは、30年前の5000倍の価格で取引されたものもあります。一時的な値下がりがあっても、数十年単位で見れば財産的価値は大きく高まるでしょう。どれだけ稀少で美しいか、自分にとってハッピーな石であるか、その点を考慮して選んでいただけると良いでしょう。

everything operates at a faster pace. In the past, it took about a month to ship goods from India to Japan, but now they can arrive in as little as two days.

The spread of the internet has dramatically transformed the way gemstone transactions are conducted. Previously, if rumors surfaced about good stones being found in remote African mines, it was not easy to travel there, and verifying the truth was difficult. However, now, images and videos of gemstones can be sent from even the most remote locations, allowing instant verification from anywhere in the world.

Differences in preferences based on countries and regions have diminished in the internet age. For example, in China, popularity was once concentrated on jade and the other "top ten gemstones." However, in recent years, awareness of garnets and tourmalines has also increased.

I believe the most critical factor in choosing colored stones in the future will be rarity. In particular, if production has stopped and only the stones already circulating in the market remain, their value will undoubtedly rise in the future. For instance, some Paraiba tourmalines have been traded at prices 5,000 times higher than 30 years ago. Even if there are temporary price drops, the financial value will significantly increase over the course of decades. When selecting, it's essential to consider how rare and beautiful the stone is and whether it brings you happiness personally.

サンディープ氏の弟ヴィシャール氏もともに宝石ビジネスに携わっている

Mr. Sandeep's younger brother, Mr.Vishal, is also involved in the jewelry business

(Clockwise from top left)
· Pt Pendant_Ethiopian Opal4.75ct,D0.70ct
· Pt Ring_Black Opal2.42ct,D1.69ct
· Pt Pendant_Black Opal11.31ct,D0.02ct
· Mexican Opal6.89 ct
· Mexican Opal14.384ct
· Boulder Opal12.00ct

# Opal

オパール

### 銀河のように光彩が煌めく驚異の美

　オパールの特徴は、なんといっても虹色の光彩があらわれる遊色効果（プレイ・オブ・カラー）です。赤、オレンジ、イエロー、緑、青、インディゴブルー、紫の七色が母岩に浮かび、その驚異の煌めきはふたつとして同じものがありません。
　オパールは古代ローマの皇帝や将軍らに愛され、王冠などにふんだんに使われました。時代が下がってもヨーロッパの宮廷での人気は高く、なかでもイギリスのビクトリア女王はいつもオパールを身に着けていたことが知られています。

### Astonishing Beauty: Sparkling Colors Like a Galaxy

The defining characteristic of opals is their play-of-color, where rainbow-like colors appear. The seven colors—red, orange, yellow, green, blue, indigo blue, and violet—float across the host rock, and no two opals share the same dazzling display.
　Ancient Roman emperors and generals cherished opals, extensively used in crowns and other adornments. Even in later periods, they remained highly popular in European courts. Notably, Queen Victoria of Britain was known to always wear opals.

Opal

*(Clockwise from the top)*
- Pt Pendant_Black Opal3.33ct,D0.75ct
- Pt Ring_Black Opal6.23ct,D3.53ct
- YG Ring_Black Opal2.31ct
- Pt Pendant_Black Opal12.42 ct,D2.402ct
- Pt Ring_Black Opal7.02ct

# Black Opal

ブラックオパール

### 黒い母岩に浮かぶ鮮烈な遊色

オパール類のなかでも頂点に輝くのがブラックオパールです。母岩が黒いことによる命名で、その黒さゆえ浮かび上がる遊色が鮮烈になり、最も高く評価されています。ブラックオパールが産出されるのは、オーストラリアのニューサウスウェールズ州ライトニングリッジのみ。発見された19世紀初めにはあまり評価されず、20世紀に入ってから注目を浴びるようになりました。

遊色効果があらわれるのは、石を構成する珪素（けいそ）（シリカ）の影響です。母岩の中に珪素の粒子が規則的に配列されることで、外から入射する光の角度が変わり、屈折して石の上に赤から紫の多彩な色があらわれます。粒子のサイズが揃っているほど輝きが増し、鮮烈な遊色効果が見られます。

石ごとに色が異なる理由は、珪素の粒子の大きさにあります。粒子のサイズによって反射する光の波長が変わり、小さいほど青色が引き立ち、大きくなるほど赤やオレンジが輝きます。

### Vivid Play-of-Color Floating on a Black Host Rock

Among the various types of opals, the one that stands at the pinnacle is the black opal. Named for its black host rock, this darkness enhances the vividness of the play-of-color, making it the most highly valued. Black opals are exclusively found in Lightning Ridge, New South Wales, Australia. When first discovered in the early 19th century, they were not highly regarded but gained attention in the 20th century.

The play-of-color effect occurs due to the influence of silica, which constitutes the stone. When silica spheres within the host rock are arranged in a regular, grid-like pattern, incoming light interacts with this structure, diffracting and producing a spectrum of colors from red to violet, visible on the stone's surface. The more uniform the particle size, the greater the brilliance and the more vivid the play-of-color effect.

The reason the colors are different for each stone is the size of the silica particles. The size affects the light that is reflected—smaller particles create more blue, while larger ones make more red and orange.

(From top to bottom)
- WG Pendant_Black Opal2.14ct,D0.36ct
- YG Pendant_Black Opal2.74ct,D0.27ct
- Pt Ring_Black Opal2.225ct,D0.85ct
- YG Ring_Black Opal1.01ct,D0.35ct

## 赤やオレンジ系が高評価

　ブラックオパールのなかで高評価を受ける石は、浮かび上がる色と遊色効果が鮮やかであるもの。色が石全体にまんべんなく分布しており、広い範囲に遊色効果が出ていることも重要です。

　色みとしては、赤やオレンジ系が入ったものが最も価値が高いと見なされます。なかでも全体に真っ赤な色が入り、その上に緋色や深紅色が鮮やかに浮かび上がる逸品は「レッド・オン・ブラック」と呼ばれます。ただし、赤が入らず、緑、青色のものにも一級品はあります。模様が独特なもの、浮かぶ色が多いものも高い評価を受けます。

　また、近年はグレーがかった母岩のなかにも、美しい色が浮かび上がるものがあります。

## Red and Orange Tones: Highly Valued

Among black opals, those with vivid emerging colors and a strong play-of-color effect are highly valued. It is also important that the colors are evenly distributed across the entire stone and that the play-of-color effect appears over a wide area.

In terms of colors, those containing red or orange tones are considered the most valuable. In particular, exceptional stones with an overall red color and vivid scarlet or deep scarlet tones on top are referred to as "Red on Black." However, first-rate stones without red tones, featuring green or blue colors, also exist. Unique patterns or stones with various emerging colors are also highly regarded.

In recent years, stones with a grayish host rock that display beautiful emerging colors have also gained attention.

(Clockwise from top left)
- Pt Pendant_Black Opal3.18ct,D0.64ct
- Pt Pendant_Black Opal4.432ct,D2.01ct
- Pt Ring_Black Opal1.45ct,D0.56ct
- Pt Ring_Black Opal1.00ct,D0.77ct
- Pt Ring_Black Opal2.93ct,D1.01ct

# Black Opal Color Grading Table

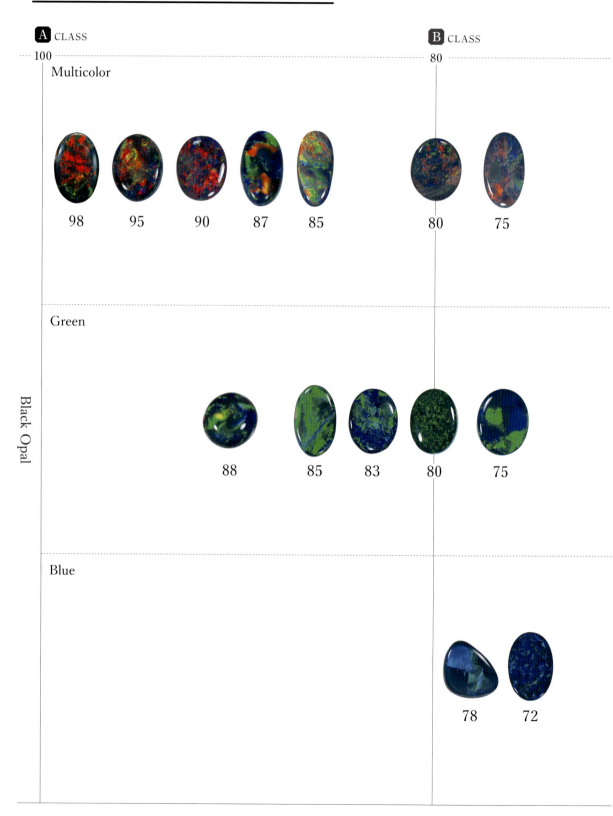

# Opal

## C CLASS

石の上の広い範囲に鮮烈な遊色効果が見られるものは最も高い評価を受けます。石の表面にくもった感じがないこと、透明感にあふれていることも重要なポイントです。

Stones that exhibit vivid play-of-color effects across a wide area on their surface receive the highest evaluation. It is also important that the stone's surface appears free of cloudiness and is filled with transparency.

### ●マルチカラー　Multicolor

マルチカラーでは多くの色がまんべんなく入っていて、特に赤やオレンジ系が際立つものほど高評価となります。100点満点に近い98点の超特級品は、燃えるような赤が全体に入って、実に神秘的な印象。87点の石は珍しい色調が目を引きますし、85点のものはオレンジに加え、黄色や緑色が入っていることが特徴です。点数が低いほど、くもった印象が目立ち、インパクトに欠けることがわかります。

In multicolor stones, those with a balanced distribution of multiple colors, especially ones where red or orange stand out, are highly valued. A super-premium stone scoring 98 out of 100 features fiery red tones throughout, giving it a truly mystical impression. A stone scoring 87 draws attention with its rare color tones, while an 85-point stone is characterized by the presence of orange along with yellow and green. Lower-scoring stones tend to appear cloudier and lack impact.

### ●グリーン　Green

赤やオレンジが入らなくとも、88点の石のように個性的な遊色が煌めくものはAクラスに位置づけられます。青いベースに入るグリーンが偏っていたり、くもっていたりすると点数が低くなります。45点の石は、Aクラス、Bクラスと比べると明らかにくもっていますが、一般的に多く流通しているのは、このタイプです。

Even if red or orange are absent, stones like the 88-point example with distinctive play-of-color brilliance are categorized as Class A. However, the score will be lower if the green within a blue base is unevenly distributed or appears cloudy. A 45-point stone, compared to Class A or Class B, is noticeably cloudier, but this type is the most commonly available in the market.

### ●ブルー　Blue

青中心の色みであっても、78点の石のようにおもしろい遊色が見られるものは、Bクラスの評価を受けます。青いベースが美しく、コントラストがはっきりしていて、広く斑が入っていることが評価のポイントです。色の出方があいまいな印象を与え、くもっている石はCクラスに分類されます。

Even with a predominantly blue color, stones like the 78-point example that exhibit interesting play-of-color are classified as Class B. The evaluation criteria include a beautiful blue base, clear contrast, and wide, evenly distributed patches of color. Stones that give an unclear impression of color distribution and appear cloudy are classified as Class C.

(From left to right)
- Boulder Opal 12.00ct
- Pt Pendant_Boulder Opal 10.148ct, D0.14ct
- Pt Ring_Boulder Opal 1.31ct, D0.47ct
- YG Ring_Boulder Opal 1.70ct, D1.67ct

# Boulder Opal

ボルダーオパール

## 評価も人気も上昇中の個性的魅力

　ボルダーオパールは茶色い鉄鉱石を母岩とするオパールです。母岩の濃淡の度合いにより遊色効果の鮮明度に違いが生じ、黒に近い母岩ではブラックオパールにも似た遊色が見られます。

　母岩に帯状に入ったオパール層に沿って研磨するため、表面が波立っている石、個性的な形をした石が多くあります。産出国はオーストラリアのみですが、鉱山は異なり、クイーンズランド州の数カ所で採掘されています。

　高評価を受けるのは、赤、オレンジ、グリーンなどの色相の石。ブルー系でも鮮やかに輝くものは高い価値が認められます。ブラックオパールの産出量の減少もあって、美しい遊色効果のあるボルダーオパールの評価は上昇しています。

## Unique Charm: Rising in Value and Popularity

Boulder opal is an opal with a brown ironstone host rock. The clarity of its play-of-color varies depending on the darkness of the host rock, with darker, nearly black host rocks exhibiting play-of-color similar to black opals.

Many stones have a unique shape and a wavy surface because they are polished along the opal layers that run in bands within the host rock. Although they are exclusively mined in Australia, the mines are spread across several locations in Queensland.

Highly valued stones include those with colors such as red, orange, and green. Even blue-toned stones with vivid brilliance are recognized for their high value. With the decline in black opal production, the value of boulder opals with beautiful play-of-color has risen.

## 乳白色に浮かぶ虹色の輝き

オパールの新たな産出地として注目されたのがエチオピア。2010年代に入りエチオピアオパールとして宝石市場に出回るようになりました。乳白色のなかに虹色の輝きが浮かび、優しい印象を醸すところが特徴です。火山活動の影響を受けて急速に形成された「火山性オパール」に属します。

角度を変えると鮮やかさが変わる輝きは非常に魅力的で、ニューフェイスながら人気を得ています。微小な穴があって水分を吸い込みやすい石なので水に濡らさないように気をつけましょう。

採掘地が現地で聖地とされる場所ゆえ、いつまで産出が続くか定かではありませんが、現在は大粒なものも購入しやすい価格です。

## Rainbow Brilliance Floating on a Milky White Background

Ethiopia has emerged as a notable new source of opals. Ethiopian opals began appearing in the gemstone market in the 2010s. They are characterized by a gentle impression, with rainbow-like brilliance floating within a milky white background. These belong to the "volcanic opals" category, which were rapidly formed due to volcanic activity.

The brightness that changes depending on the angle is incredibly attractive, making them a popular newcomer to the market. However, as the stones have microscopic pores and tend to absorb moisture, care should be taken to avoid getting them wet.

The locals consider the mining location sacred, so it is uncertain how long production will continue. Currently, however, even large stones are available at accessible prices.

(From left to right)
- YG Pendant_Ethiopian Opal15.94ct, D0.06ct
- WG Pendant_Ethiopian Opal4.34ct, D0.146ct
- WG Pendant_Ethiopian Opal2.98ct, D0.71ct

# Ethiopian Opal

エチオピアオパール

## Color variations

遊色効果の高さをいろいろな角度からチェック。斑の色全体のバランスが良いものが高い評価を受けます。

Check the quality of the play-of-color from various angles. Stones with well-balanced colors throughout the patches receive higher evaluations.

(From top to bottom)
- Pt Pendant_Mexican Opal10.29ct,D17.60ct
- YG Pendant_Mexican Opal8.30ct,Dragon Garnet0.48ct
- Pt Ring_Mexican Opal2.09ct,D0.45ct
- Pt Ring_Mexican Opal2.32ct,D0.815ct
- Pt Ring_Mexican Opal1.25ct,D0.51ct

## Color variations

Fire Opal

Water Opal

ファイヤーオパールは、赤、オレンジ、黄色、緑などが鮮やかなことが重要ポイント。ウォーターオパールも、ブルーに赤やオレンジが浮き出ているものが高評価。

For fire opals, vibrancy in colors such as red, orange, yellow, and green is a key factor. Those with red or orange appearing on a blue base are highly valued for water opals.

# Mexican Opal

メキシコオパール

### 炎を思わせるファイヤーオパール

　その名の通り、メキシコで産出されるメキシコオパール。見る角度により炎のような赤やオレンジの遊色があらわれるものは、ファイヤーオパールと呼ばれます。メソアメリカの歴史のなかで、守護石、権力の象徴として珍重されました。大航海時代にスペインに征服されて以降は、ヨーロッパに送られた多くの石が王侯貴族に愛されました。

　最も有名なメキシコオパールは、フランス皇帝ナポレオンがジョセフィーヌ妃に贈った逸品。冠につけられ、「トロイの炎」と呼ばれました。

　ファイヤーオパールとは対照的に、涼やかなブルー系のウォーターオパールもあります。

　評価のポイントは遊色の鮮やかさと透明度。真紅の発色が鮮烈な石は大変価値が高くなります。

### Fire Opal: Reminiscent of Flames

As its name suggests, Mexican opal is mined in Mexico. Stones that display fiery red or orange play-of-color reminiscent of flames, depending on the viewing angle, are called fire opals. In Mesoamerican history, they were treasured as protective stones and symbols of power. After the Spanish conquest during the Age of Exploration, many of these stones were sent to Europe and adored by royalty and aristocrats.

　The most famous Mexican opal is "The Burning of Troy," which French Emperor Napoleon gifted to his wife, Empress Josephine. It was set into a crown.

　In contrast to fire opals, there are also cool-toned blue water opals.

　Key evaluation points are the vibrancy of the play-of-color and the transparency. Stones with vivid crimson colors are considered exceptionally valuable.

# Opal
## Production Trends and Value
オパールの産出動向とその価値

ブラックオパールは、オーストラリア南東部に位置するニューサウスウェルズ州北部のライトニングリッジという小さな町近辺でのみ産出されます。産出量は減少傾向が続いています（詳しくはp.60参照）。同じオーストラリア産のボルダーオパールは、ニューサウスウェルズ州の北側にあるクイーンズランド州一帯の半乾燥地帯で採掘されています。やはり産出量は減少傾向にあります。

エチオピアオパールは、エチオピア北西部のアムハラ州で産出されます。現在も安定的に流通していますが、大きなサイズの美しいものは少なくなってきています。

メキシコオパールの主な産出地はメキシコのハリスコ州マグダレーナです。クリアなウォーター系は近年ほとんど産出しておらず、現在流通しているのは過去にフリーフォームでカットされていた石をカボションに再研磨したものが多く、数は減っています。以前は3カラット以上のものも多くありましたが、近年は1カラット程度がほとんどで、大きいものの稀少価値は高まっています。

ファイヤー系のメキシコオパールは、ウォーター系と比べると安定的に流通していますが、美しく斑の出るものは少なく、こちらも大きいサイズのものは減ってきています。

Black opals are exclusively mined in the vicinity of Lightning Ridge, a small town located in northern New South Wales, southeastern Australia. The production volume has been on a declining trend (see p. 60 for details). Similarly, boulder opals, also from Australia, are mined in the semi-arid regions of Queensland, which lies to the north of New South Wales. Their production is also steadily decreasing.

Ethiopian opals are sourced from the Amhara region in northwestern Ethiopia. While they remain steadily available in the market, large, high-quality specimens have become increasingly rare.

The primary source of Mexican opals is Magdalena in the state of Jalisco, Mexico. Clear, water-type opals have become scarce in recent years, and many of the stones currently available are older pieces that have been re-polished from freeform cuts into cabochons. Their numbers are decreasing. In the past, 3-carat or larger stones were common, but today, most pieces are around 1 carat, making larger specimens significantly more valuable.

Fire-type Mexican opals, in contrast to water-types, are more consistently available. However, pieces with beautiful color distribution are rare, and large-sized stones have also become less common.

私はオーストラリアのライトニングリッジに居を構え、ブラックオパールを採掘して日本や香港、アメリカなどに卸売をしています。40年ほど前にシドニーのオパールの会社で働き始め、20年して独立しました。ライトニングリッジに移ったのは、産出量が減り、自分も採掘しつつ、ほかからも買い付ける体制にするため。夏場は50℃にもなる酷暑ゆえ、日本と季節が逆になるオーストラリアでは3月〜11月はじめが採掘の時期です。

良質のブラックオパールの産出量は、20、30年前の50分の1から100分の1くらいまで激減しました。町の人口もピーク時の約1万5000人の3分の1くらいでしょうか。鉱物資源は良質のものが出る鉱区から効率よく掘り、出なくなると次へ移ります。良い鉱区がうまく見つからない

と、第二の選択肢、第三の選択肢となり、良質の石が少なくなります。たくさん採れないと採掘にまわす費用も出せず、事業が小規模になります。

採掘にあたっては、まずあちこち掘ってみるためにプロスペクトライセンスという試掘許可をとり、出そうなところを見つけたら一般ライセンスをとって本格的に掘ります。個人では50m四方を2区画までできます。基本的に2〜4人でパートナーとなり、石が採れたら利益を山分けします。

近年の最大の障壁は、ニューサウスウェルズ州の環境関連の規制です。以前のようにあちこち試掘できたら良い鉱区が見つかる可能性もありますが、場所を限定され、厳しくなる一方。オパールも石炭や鉄鉱石の採掘と同じ鉱業として環境保全のルールが適用され、州政府は経済効果が少ない

Located in Lightning Ridge, Australia, I mine and wholesale black opals to markets in Japan, Hong Kong, and the United States. About 40 years ago, I started my career at an opal company in Sydney and became independent after 20 years. I relocated to Lightning Ridge to address the decline in production, enabling me to mine opals myself while also sourcing them from others. The mining season in Lightning Ridge runs from March to early November, which corresponds to autumn and winter in the southern hemisphere, avoiding the intense summer heat that can reach up to 50℃.

The production of high-quality black opals has decreased dramatically, to about 1/50 or even 1/100 the amount produced 20–30 years ago. The town's population has also dropped to roughly one-third of its peak of 15,000 residents. Mineral resources are mined systematically, starting with areas that yield

high-quality opals. Once these deposits are exhausted, miners move on to the next site. If good mining areas cannot be found, they are forced to turn to second or third options, resulting in fewer high-quality stones. Limited production also means less funding for mining, causing operations to scale down.

To start mining, prospectors first obtain a prospecting license to test various areas. When a promising site is found, they acquire a general license for full-scale mining. Individuals are allowed to manage up to two claims, each measuring 50 meters square. Typically, two to four partners work together, sharing profits from the opals they extract.

In recent years, the greatest obstacle has been environmental regulations in New South Wales. In the past, being able to prospect in multiple areas

# Interview

### Profile

オパール輸出卸売業者
## 蓑田秀一氏
**Opal Export and Wholesale Dealer**
**Mr. Shu Minoda**

1983年大学卒業後に渡豪。メルボルンでオパール会社に入社。1985年同社のシドニー本社に移りバイヤー兼卸売りを担当。2003年退社後に、オパール輸出卸売会社 イリスオパールを設立。主にアメリカ、日本、香港、中国のトレードショーに出展、販売をする。2015年ライトニングリッジに移住しブラックオパールの採掘を始め現在に至る。

# ライトニングリッジのブラックオパール産地動向

## The Latest Trends in Lightning Ridge's Black Opal Production

蓑田氏の鉱区にて、岡本代表が坑道の壁に電動ドリルを入れているところ
At Mr. Minoda's mining site, President Okamoto is drilling into the tunnel wall with a power drill

地上から穴を掘り、地下10メートルのところに採掘場がある
The mining site is 10 meters underground, accessible by digging from the surface

After graduating from university in 1983, Shu Minoda moved to Australia and joined an opal company in Melbourne. In 1985, he transferred to the Sydney headquarters as a buyer and managed wholesale operations. After leaving the company in 2003, he founded IRIS OPAL PTY LTD, an opal export and wholesale company, exhibiting and selling at trade shows in the United States, Japan, Hong Kong, and China. In 2015, he relocated to Lightning Ridge and has been mining black opals ever since.

## 市場の拡大と母岩の色の変化
### Expanding Markets and Changes in Host Rock Colors

事業は継続させない方針まで打ち出しています。

私のところではパートナーが研磨をしています。ブラックオパールの研磨は他の色石とはまったく勝手が異なり難しく、彼の60年を超える経験と技術を継承しないといけないのですが、産出量が減って成り手がなく困っています。

ほかのオパールも同様に厳しい状況です。クイーンズランド州ではボルダーオパールの良い鉱区が集まる地域を州立公園にする計画があり、近いうちに掘れなくなりそうです。サウスオーストラリア州クーパーピディでのホワイトオパールの産出もかなり減っています。エチオピアでオパールが発見され、10年ほど大人気になった間に需要が落ち込み、採掘業者が減ったことが影響しています。

良品の産出が減っている一方、新しい動きも見られます。そのひとつがコロナ禍以降、ライトニングリッジを訪れる旅行客が増えたこと。州境を超えた移動が禁じられるなか、州内から訪れた人たちから「面白い」との評判が広まりました。

コロナ禍でSNSで盛んに拡散され、認知度と客層が広がったこともあります。客足が途絶えていた小売業の方々が商品の画像をたくさん載せるようになり、「こんなきれいな石があるとは」と反響を呼んだのです。

特に、市場が拡大したのが、中東、中国、東南

研磨をしている蓑田氏とそのパートナー
Mr. Minoda and his partner polishing an opal

increased the chances of discovering high-quality deposits. However, stricter rules have now restricted locations, and the situation continues to grow more challenging. Opal mining is subject to the same environmental preservation rules as coal and iron ore mining. The state government has even announced a policy that operations with low economic impact may not be permitted to continue.

My partner is responsible for cutting and polishing opals. Cutting black opals requires a completely different skill set compared to other gemstones, and it is extremely challenging. His expertise, developed over more than 60 years, must be passed down. However, with declining production and no successors in sight, we are struggling with this issue.

Other types of opals are facing similarly dire situations. In Queensland, areas known for high-quality boulder opals are being designated as state parks, which means mining in those areas will likely be prohibited soon. In Coober Pedy, South Australia, the production of white opals has also significantly declined. The popularity of newly discovered opals in Ethiopia, which lasted about a decade, has pushed down the demand for Australian opals. This further reduced the number of miners, one of the key factors for the decline.

While the production of high-quality black opals continues to decline, there have been some notable developments in recent years.

One significant change is the increase in visitors to Lightning Ridge since the COVID-19 pandemic. With interstate travel restricted, people from within the state began exploring the region, and word quickly spread about its fascinating appeal.

Social media also played a key role during the

**Interview** Mr. Shu Minoda

アジア。中東では男性がカフスボタンなどに仕立てることが多くあります。ただ、ネットの画像だけを見て購入するケースも多く、届いたら色が違うというトラブルはかなり起きています。

中国では日本同様、少し小さくてもきれいなものが好まれる傾向があります。日本ではブルーグリーンや赤が入ったものが好まれますが、中国では人それぞれですね。

そもそもブラックオパールの人気は、アメリカで火がつき、バブル期の日本に広まりました。日本ではホワイトオパールが根づいていたので、受け入れる素地ができていたといえるでしょう。アメリカではブルーグリーン、赤い色、そして色が少しあまくとも大きめのものが好まれます。

現在の傾向として、母岩の色が少し薄くなってきています。濃いほうが色が強く出ますが、多少薄くとも遊色効果の美しい石もありますし、好みの問題もありますね。濃い色のものは数がとても少ないだけに、価格は高くなります。

ブラックオパールは非常に稀な条件がそろって生まれるもの。分子が規則正しく並ぶ非結晶質で、非常に特殊な鉱物です。これほど複雑でバラエティ豊かな宝石はほかにないでしょう。市場が拡がる一方で産出量はまるで追いつかず、稀少性は高まっています。ここ５、６年で２、３倍に値上がりしていますが、稀少性の高いほかの宝石と比べたらまだまだです。さらに価格が上昇する可能性が高いと思われます。

ブラックオパールの原石
Rough black opal

研磨途中のブラックオパール
Black opal being polished

pandemic, raising awareness and broadening the customer base. Retailers, whose businesses had stalled due to a lack of foot traffic, started sharing images of their gemstones online. These posts garnered widespread attention, with many commenting, "I didn't know such beautiful stones existed."

The market has particularly expanded in the Middle East, China, and Southeast Asia.

In the Middle East, black opals are often crafted into cufflinks for men. However, many buyers rely solely on online images, which has led to frequent disputes when the delivered stones differ in color from what was shown online.

In China, as in Japan, slightly smaller yet beautiful stones are generally preferred. Japanese consumers tend to favor stones with blue-green hues or hints of red, while preferences in China vary significantly from person to person.

The global popularity of black opals initially began in the United States before spreading to Japan during the economic bubble era.

Japan already had an appreciation for white opals, which likely helped pave the way for black opals to gain a foothold. In the United States, blue-green and red hues are highly sought after, as well as larger stones, even if their colors are slightly softer.

Currently, one noticeable trend is that the base color of the host rock is becoming lighter. Darker bases produce more intense colors, but lighter bases can also come with good play-of-color, contributing to the diversity of various preferences. Meanwhile, darker stones remain far rarer and significantly more expensive.

Black opals are formed under extremely rare conditions, making them one of the most extraordinary gemstones in existence.

Their unique non-crystalline structure, with molecules arranged in an orderly pattern, sets them apart. No other gemstone combines such complexity and diversity. While the market for black opals continues to expand, production cannot keep pace, further increasing their rarity. Over the past five to six years, prices have doubled or even tripled. That said, compared to other highly rare gemstones, the price increase of black opals has been relatively modest, and it is likely that prices will continue to rise.

(Clockwise from top left)
- Pt Ring_Star Sapphire6.52ct,D1.82ct
- Pt Pendant_Orange Sapphire4.00ct,D1.41ct
- Pt Ring_Pink Sapphire1.57ct,D1.87ct
- Pt Ring_Blue Sapphire8.02ct,D3.80ct
- Pt Ring_Padparadscha Sapphire2.12ct,D2.75ct
- YG Ring_Golden Sapphire5.00ct,D1.66ct

# Sapphire

サファイア

## 青に加えて豊富な色相

　古代から珍重され、神に近い高貴な石として数々の伝説に彩られてきたサファイア。古代ペルシャではサファイアこそが大地を支える石であり、そのどこまでも深い青が天空に反映され、青空が形成されていると信じられていたといいます。

　サファイアの語源はラテン語の「青」。神秘的な青い石というイメージが強いものの、他の色もあります。ピンク、オレンジ、イエロー、グリーンなど豊富な色相があり、これらはまとめてファンシーカラーサファイアと呼ばれます。

## A Rich Variety of Colors Beyond Blue

Sapphire, highly valued since ancient times, has been adorned with numerous legends as a noble stone close to the divine. In ancient Persia, sapphire was believed to be the stone supporting the earth, and its deep blue color was reflected in the sky, forming the blue heavens.

　The word "sapphire" originates from the Latin term for "blue." While it is strongly associated with the image of a mysterious blue stone, sapphires also come in other colors. Pink, orange, yellow, green, and other colors are collectively referred to as fancy-colored sapphires.

# Blue Sapphire

ブルーサファイア

## 最高級品はコーンフラワーブルーとロイヤルブルー

　さまざまなカラーバリエーションがあるサファイアのなかでも、最も高く評価されるのはブルーサファイアです。青の色合いによって見出される価値が大きく異なります。

　最上の評価を得るのは、コーンフラワーブルーと呼ばれる青。コーンフラワーとは矢車菊（セントーレア）のことで、その花のような深い青をしています。インドのカシミール地方が有名な産出地ですが、近年はほとんど産出されず、幻の石となっています。一方、ロイヤルブルーサファイアは、イギリス王室がミャンマー産のブルーサファイアに対してつけた名称。イギリス王室の公式のロイヤルブルーと同じく、深みがある青色でやや紫がかっているのが特徴です。

## Cornflower Blue and Royal Blue: The Finest Quality Pieces

Among the various color variations of sapphire, blue sapphire is the most highly valued. Its worth varies greatly depending on the shade of blue.

The highest-rated shade is known as cornflower blue. Cornflower refers to the blue of the cornflower blossom, a deep and vivid shade of blue. The Kashmir region of India is a renowned source of this gemstone, but in recent years, production has virtually ceased, making it a legendary rarity.

On the other hand, Royal Blue Sapphire is a name given by the British royal family to blue sapphires from Myanmar. It shares the characteristics of the official royal blue of the British monarchy, featuring a rich, deep blue with a slightly purplish color.

*(Clockwise from left)*
- *Pt Ring_Blue Sapphire4.83ct,D1.16ct*
- *Pt Ring_Cab Blue Sapphire4.13ct*
- *Pt Ring_Blue Sapphire5.33ct,D2.02ct*
- *Pt Ring_Blue Sapphire4.24ct,D1.22ct*
- *Blue Sapphire 10.64ct*

### 聖職者、権力者に愛される石

　ブルーサファイアが神に近い石としてヨーロッパでいかに信仰と結びついていたかは、旧約聖書に登場することからもわかります。シナイ山でモーゼが神から授けられた十戒は、青いサファイアに刻まれていたといわれます。

　高貴な青色の石は、時代を超え聖職者に好まれました。中世から近世にかけてのキリスト教会では、ブルーサファイアのリングをつけると、神の意志をこの世に伝えることができると信じられたため、ローマ教皇、枢機卿たちはこぞって大粒の石のついたリングを手に入れました。

　ブルーサファイアは時の権力者にも愛されました。ヨーロッパ各国の宮廷でもてはやされ、王室は権力の象徴たる王冠に逸品を用いました。

　現在では、良質のブルーサファイアは稀少価値が高く、それだけ価格も上がっています。特Aクラスの逸品はほとんど市場に出ることもなく、大変高額となっています。

### A Gemstone Beloved by Priests and Kings

The connection between blue sapphire and faith in Europe as a stone close to God is evident from its mention in the Old Testament. It is said that the Ten Commandments given to Moses by God on Mount Sinai were engraved on blue sapphire.

　The noble blue gemstone has been favored by priests across the ages. From the Middle Ages to the early modern period, in the Christian Church, wearing a blue sapphire ring was believed to enable one to convey the will of God to the world. For this reason, the Pope and cardinals sought to obtain rings with large sapphire stones.

　Blue sapphire was also cherished by kings of the time. It was highly prized in the royal courts of Europe, and royal families used exquisite pieces in their crowns as symbols of power.

　Today, high-quality blue sapphires are exceedingly rare, driving their prices even higher. Very top-grade pieces are almost never seen on the market and are extremely expensive.

*(From top to bottom)*
- *Pt Ring_Blue Sapphire4.00ct,D1.40ct*
- *Pt Ring_Blue Sapphire5.04ct,D1.20ct*
- *Pt Ring_Blue Sapphire2.74ct,D0.45ct*

# Star Sapphire

スターサファイア

## 神秘的な六条の線が浮かび上がる

　ブルーサファイアのなかで、カボションにカットを施すと六条の線が浮かび上がり、まるで星のように見える石をスターサファイアといいます。稀少性が高く、サファイアのなかでも特別な位置づけがなされ、それだけ高額です。

　スターサファイアは古くから世界中で特別な力を宿す石として信奉されました。キリスト教の聖職者が六条の線を信頼、希望、運命のあらわれと捉えたほか、ヨーロッパでは広く幸運を呼び込む石として珍重されました。

　六条の線が浮かび上がる特別な現象は、内包物が針状に入り込み、石の六角柱面に平行するように走っている場合に起こります。これをアステリズム効果、一般にはスター効果といいます。

　アステリズム効果が見られるのはブルーサファイアに限らず、バイオレットサファイアとイエローサファイアにもスターサファイアがあります。ただし、イエローは特にレアでほぼ出回りません。

*(From top to bottom)*
- *Pt/YG Ring_Violet Star Sapphire22.50ct,D2.63ct*
- *Pt Ring_Star Sapphire8.88ct,D3.80ct*
- *Pt Ring_Star Sapphire4.77ct,D0.51ct*
- *Pt Ring_Star Sapphire6.62ct,D1.19ct*

## Mystical Six-Rayed Lines Appear

Among blue sapphires, those that reveal six-rayed lines when cut into a cabochon shape and appear like stars are called star sapphires. They are highly rare and hold a special status among sapphires, making them correspondingly expensive.

　Star sapphires have long been revered worldwide as stones possessing special powers. Christian priests interpreted the six-rayed lines as symbols of faith, hope, and destiny, while in Europe, they were widely cherished as stones that bring good fortune.

　The unique phenomenon of six-rayed lines appearing occurs when needle-like inclusions are aligned parallel to the planes of the hexagonal crystal structure of the stone. This is known as asterism, commonly called the star effect.

　Asterism is not limited to blue sapphires; violet and yellow sapphires can also form star sapphires. However, yellow star sapphires are especially rare and almost never seen on the market.

# Sapphire Color Grading Table

# Sapphire

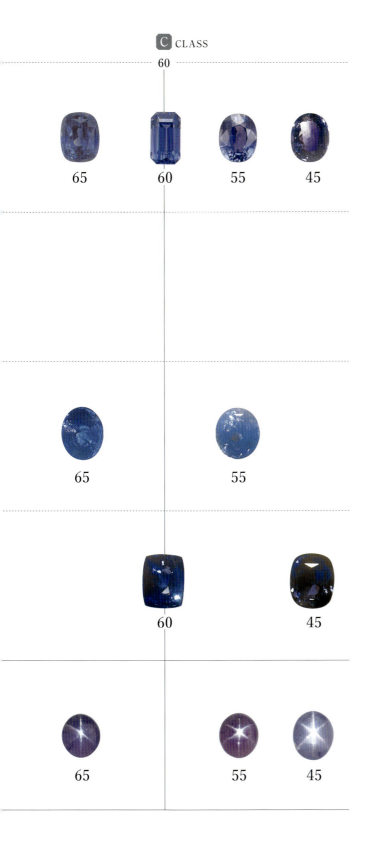

青い色の美しさに加え、くもりない輝きと内包物を評価します。サファイアは内包物が多いため、目立つ場所にあって美しさを損ねている場合でなければ、大幅な減点対象にする必要はありません。

In addition to the beauty of its blue color, the clarity of its brilliance and inclusions are evaluated. Since sapphires tend to have many inclusions, they do not need to be heavily penalized unless the inclusions are in prominent locations that detract from their beauty.

● ブルーサファイア　Blue Sapphire

深い青色が高く評価されますが、タイ産のように黒みを感じさせる色合いでは評価が下がります。95点のマダガスカル産カットサファイアは、最高級のカシミール産を思わせる深い色合いと輝き。隣りの92点の石も内包物がほとんどなく、輝きが際立っています。スリランカ産のカットサファイアは、深い色合い、透明感のある内面からの輝き、テリが美しいものが高い点数を得ています。スリランカ産のカボションサファイアは、透明感とテリ、やさしい色の逸品がAクラスと評価されています。色みが浅く、輝きと透明感に欠け、内包物が目立つものは評価が低くなります。

Deep blue colors are highly valued, but darker tones, such as those from Thailand, are rated lower. A 95-point cut sapphire from Madagascar features a deep color and brilliance reminiscent of the finest Kashmir sapphires. A 92-point stone also stands out with its minimal inclusions and exceptional brilliance. Cut sapphires from Sri Lanka score high points for their deep coloration, inner brilliance with transparency, and beautiful luster. Cabochon sapphires from Sri Lanka are rated as Class A for their transparency, luster, and gentle colors. Those with pale coloration, lacking brilliance and transparency, or with noticeable inclusions are rated lower.

● スターサファイア　Star Sapphire

色と輝きに加えて、六条の線の出方が重要ポイントです。95点の石は、深みのあるインクブルーにきれいに線が入った特級品です。深い色でアステリズム効果がはっきりあらわれた石はきわめてレアです。線の一部があいまいであったり、バランスがとれていない入り方であったり、表面にシルク状の内包物が見えたりするものは、評価が下がります。バイオレットのスターサファイアについても、色が美しく、六条の線がきれいに出ていれば、一級品として評価されます。

In addition to color and brilliance, the clarity of the six-rayed lines is a crucial factor. A 95-point stone is a top-grade specimen with deep ink-blue coloration and sharply defined lines. Stones with deep colors and a clearly visible asterism are extremely rare. However, stones with partially blurred or unbalanced lines, or those with visible silk-like inclusions on the surface, are rated lower. For violet star sapphires, stones with beautiful colors and clearly defined six-rayed lines are also highly rated as premium-quality pieces.

069

*(From top to bottom)*
- Pt Ring_Padparadscha Sapphire8.71ct,D2.72ct
- YG Ring_Padparadscha Sapphire2.21ct,D1.05ct
- Pt Ring_Padparadscha Sapphire4.22ct,D1.25ct
- Pt Ring_Padparadscha Sapphire6.64ct,D2.85ct
- Pt Pendant_Padparadscha Sapphire3.49ct,D1.20ct

Sapphire

# Padparadscha Sapphire

パパラチアサファイア

(From top to bottom)
- Pt Ring_Padparadscha Sapphire1.11ct,D0.58ct
- WG Ring_Padparadscha Sapphire1.81ct,D0.746ct
- Pt Ring_Padparadscha Sapphire1.796ct,D0.50ct
- Pt Ring_Padparadscha Sapphire1.10ct,D0.41ct
- Pt Ring_Padparadscha Sapphire0.75ct,D0.73ct

## 気品あふれる"サファイアの王様"

ブルー以外の色のファンシーカラーサファイアのなかで最も高く評価されるのが、パパラチアサファイアです。ブルーサファイアと並んで「キング・オブ・サファイア（サファイアの王様）」と形容されます。

パパラチアとは、スリランカの言葉で「蓮の花」という意味。ピンクとオレンジの中間の蓮の花に似た色合いが気品ある印象を醸し、独特の魅力となっています。オレンジ系が強いものからピンクに近いものまで、幅広い色相があります。

良質の石の産出はごく一部に限られ、色の薄いものがほとんどを占めます。稀少性が非常に高いパパラチアの逸品には、Aクラスのブルーサファイアを上回る高額のものもあります。

## The Graceful "King of Sapphires"

Among the fancy-colored sapphires that are not blue, the most highly valued is the padparadscha sapphire. Alongside blue sapphire, it is described as the "King of Sapphires."

The term "padparadscha" originates from a Sri Lankan word meaning "lotus flower." Its pink-orange color, resembling a lotus blossom, exudes a sense of elegance and unique charm. The color spectrum ranges from stronger orange tones to shades closer to pink.

The production of high-quality stones is extremely limited, with the majority being lighter in color. Exceptional padparadscha sapphires, due to their rarity, can command prices even higher than Class A blue sapphires.

# Pink Sapphire

ピンクサファイア

## 可憐なピンクの輝き

　可憐ななかに華やいだ印象があり、女性に人気が高いピンクサファイア。パステルカラーの淡いピンクから、赤みの強いピンクまで幅広い色相があります。

　色合いの違いは、クロムなど金属元素の入り方によるものです。サファイアは鉱物としてはコランダムという名称で、ルビーも同じくコランダム。ルビーに近い色のピンクサファイアもあります。

　ピンクサファイアを含むファンシーカラーの輝きを楽しめるようになったのは、中世以降のこと。カッティング技術の飛躍的向上により、原石にファセットと呼ばれる面をいくつもつくり出し、豊かな色彩の美を引き出せるようになりました。

## Lovely and Sweet Pink

Pink sapphires, with their delicate yet glamorous impression, are highly popular among women. Their colors range widely from soft pastel pinks to deep pinks with strong red tones.

　The color variations are due to the inclusion of metallic elements such as chromium. Sapphires are a type of mineral known as corundum, as are rubies. Some pink sapphires even have colors close to rubies.

　Enjoying the brilliance of pink sapphires and other fancy colors became possible after the Middle Ages. With the remarkable advancements in cutting techniques, facets—flat surfaces—were skillfully created on rough stones, revealing the rich beauty of their colors.

*(Clockwise from top left)*
- Pt Ring_Pink Sapphire1.43 ct,D0.62ct
- Pt Ring_Pink Sapphire1.82ct,D0.26ct
- Pink Sapphire6.72ct
- Pink Sapphire3.20ct

## 個性あふれる生き生きした力強さ

　エネルギーあふれる強さ、際立つ個性を感じさせるのがオレンジサファイアの魅力。オレンジの色が濃いほど高く評価されます。

　オレンジサファイアはもともとスリランカで産出されていました。フルーツのオレンジのような生き生きした印象で、濃いオレンジに輝く一級品が市場に供給されていました。

　1999年になって透明度が非常に高く、夕日のような赤に近い鮮烈なオレンジサファイアがマダガスカルで発見され、たちまち人気を博しました。

　近年はいずれも産出量が減り、特に赤みが強く深いオレンジサファイアはほとんど流通していない状況です。品薄ゆえ価格も高騰が続いています。

### Vivid and Dynamic Orange

The charm of orange sapphires lies in their energetic strength and striking individuality. The deeper the orange color, the higher they are valued.

　Orange sapphires were originally mined in Sri Lanka. They evoke a lively impression, like a ripe orange fruit, with premium-quality pieces of rich, vibrant orange brilliance having been supplied to the market.

　In 1999, a highly transparent and vivid orange sapphire, resembling the red colors of a sunset, was discovered in Madagascar and quickly gained popularity.

　In recent years, production has decreased across the board, and particularly those with strong red and deep orange colors are rarely seen in the market. Due to their scarcity, prices have continued to rise.

*(From left to right)*
・Pt Pendant_Orange Sapphire1.00ct,D0.08ct
・Orange Sapphire7.63ct
・Pt Pendant_Orange Sapphire3.47ct,D0.188ct
・YG Pendant_Orange Sapphire3.06ct,D0.10ct

# Orange Sapphire

オレンジサファイア

(From top left to right)
- Pt Ring_Yellow Sapphire1.662ct,D0.21ct
- Pt Ring_Yellow Sapphire4.76ct,D1.94ct
- YG Pendant_Golden Sapphire8.03ct,D0.249ct
- Pt Ring_Yellow Sapphire1.691ct,D0.38ct

# Golden Sapphire & Yellow Sapphire

ゴールデンサファイア & イエローサファイア

### 注目度が上がるイエローの煌めき

　黄色い色みのサファイアは、イエローサファイアと総称されます。赤や褐色を帯びた色合いからレモンのように薄い色まで幅広い色相があり、運気を呼ぶ黄色の人気から価格も上がっています。

　一方、褐色からオレンジ色がかった濃い色と強い輝きを特徴とするのが、ゴールデンサファイア。非常にレアで、入手困難です。

　両者の鑑別は大変難しく、海外ではゴールデンサファイアがイエローまたはオレンジに分類されていることも多くあります。暗い場所で紫外線ライトを当て、蛍光色に光るものをゴールデンと見なすこともありますが、世界的に統一された基準ではありません。

### Yellow and Gold Brilliance

Yellow-colored sapphires are generally referred to as yellow sapphires. Their colors range widely from reddish or brownish tones to pale lemon-like shades. Due to the popularity of yellow as a color that brings good fortune, their prices are also rising.

　Meanwhile, golden sapphires are characterized by their deep colors, which range from brownish to orange colors, and their strong brilliance. They are extremely rare and difficult to obtain.

　Distinguishing between the two is very challenging. In many countries, golden sapphires are often categorized as either yellow or orange. Some may consider those that glow under ultraviolet light in a dark place as golden, but this is not a globally standardized criterion.

# Green Sapphire & Violet Sapphire & Bicolor Sapphire

グリーンサファイア & バイオレットサファイア & バイカラーサファイア

(Clockwise from left)
- Pt Pendant_Violet Sapphire4.89ct
- Green Sapphire10.678ct
- Green Sapphire13.47ct

## 緑や紫、2色のサファイア

グリーンサファイアの色には幅があり、最高評価を受けるのは明るく輝く美しい緑です。そのような色は非常に稀で、ほとんどはオリーブ色。黒っぽく暗い色調です。ごく一部に、内包物によりアステリズム効果が見られるものがあります。

青みがかった紫のサファイアは、バイオレットサファイアといいます。赤みが強い紫の場合はパープルサファイアと呼んで、区別することもあります。産出量が少なく、稀少性が高く、これから人気となりそうです。

一方、2色に分かれたサファイアはバイカラーサファイアといいます。組み合わせとして多いのは、緑と黄色。レアなのは青と紫で、中央で明確に色が分かれたものは非常に高く評価されます。

## Green, Purple, and Bi-Colored Sapphires

The color of green sapphires varies widely, with the highest-rated ones glowing in a brilliant, beautiful green. Such colors are extremely rare; most are olive-toned, appearing dark and muted. A tiny proportion exhibits asterism due to inclusions.

Bluish-purple sapphires are called violet sapphires. When the purple has a strong reddish color, they are sometimes distinguished as purple sapphires. Their production is limited, making them highly rare, and they are likely to gain popularity in the future.

Meanwhile, sapphires divided into two colors are called bicolor sapphires. The most common combination is green and yellow. The rarer pairing is blue and purple, and those with a clear separation of colors in the center are highly valued.

(Clockwise from top left)
- Bicolor Sapphire2.75ct・Bicolor Sapphire0.52ct
- Bicolor Sapphire0.73ct・Bicolor Sapphire0.70ct
- Bicolor Sapphire0.72ct

# Fancy-Colored Sapphire Grading Table

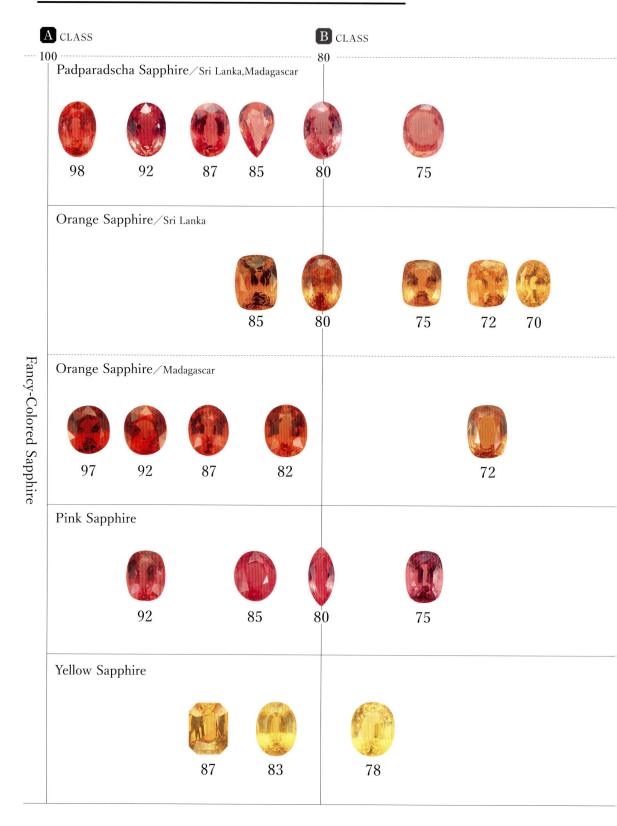

# Sapphire

ファンシーカラーを評価するポイントは、ブルーサファイアと同じく色、内包物、輝きの3点。色は濃くなるほど評価が高くなります。ただし、黒みを帯びた色合いになると、黒さの度合いに応じて評価が下がります。内包物はサファイアはもともと多いため、美しさを損なわない限り、特に大きな減点対象とはなりません。

The key points for evaluating fancy-colored gemstones, similar to blue sapphires, are color, inclusions, and brilliance. The color is rated higher as it becomes more profound and more intense. Conversely, the evaluation decreases as the degree of blackness increases. Regarding inclusions, sapphires are naturally prone to having them, and as long as they do not significantly detract from the gemstone's beauty, they are not considered a major factor for deduction.

### ● パパラチアサファイア  Padparadscha Sapphire

98点はまさに蓮の花の色の最高級品。色、透明感とも申し分ないスリランカ産です。微妙に色が異なる92点の石はマダガスカル産。色が浅く、テリが少なくなるほどに評価が下がります。

A 98-point gemstone is the finest grade, exhibiting the color of a lotus flower at its best. Its color and transparency are impeccable, and it originates from Sri Lanka. A 92-point gemstone, with a slightly different color, comes from Madagascar. As the color becomes lighter and the luster diminishes, the evaluation score decreases accordingly.

### ● オレンジサファイア  Orange Sapphire

97点の石はレッドオレンジが典型的なマダガスカル産。色、テリ、透明感と三拍子そろった最高級品です。スリランカ産のオレンジサファイアは、マダガスカル産とは異なる色み。深みとテリがあるものがAクラスの評価を受けます。いずれも色が浅くなるほど評価が下がりますが、透明度が高く美しく輝くものは色が薄くとも良質と見なされます。

A 97-point gemstone is a typical red-orange sapphire from Madagascar, representing a top-grade piece with excellent color, luster, and transparency. Orange sapphires from Sri Lanka exhibit a different color. Those with a depth of color and strong luster receive an A-grade evaluation. In both cases, the evaluation score decreases as the color becomes lighter. However, gemstones with high clarity and beautiful brilliance are considered high-quality, even if their color is pale.

### ● ピンクサファイア  Pink Sapphire

ピンクの深み、眩い輝きがよくあらわれているのが、92点の特級品。Cクラスに位置づけられた石は、色が薄すぎ、紫がかっているのがわかります。

A 92-point gemstone, classified as a top-grade piece, showcases a deep pink color and dazzling brilliance. In contrast, gemstones categorized as C-class exhibit colors that are too pale or have a noticeable purplish tint.

### ● イエローサファイア  Yellow Sapphire

87点の石は、美しい黄色にオレンジみが少し加わった一級品。隣りの83点の石は、レモンイエローの透明感にあふれ、さわやかな輝きが印象的です。色が薄くなるほど評価が下がります。

An 87-point gemstone is a first-grade piece, showcasing a beautiful yellow color with a slight hint of orange. In comparison, the 83-point gemstone features a transparent lemon-yellow color with an impressively fresh brilliance. As the color becomes lighter, the evaluation score decreases.

# Sapphire
## Production Trends and Value
サファイアの産出動向とその価値

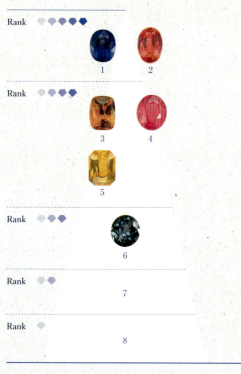

### Rank by Type

❶ **Blue Sapphire**
Sri Lanka／Thailand／
Madagascar／Myanmar／
South Africa／Namibia／
Nigeria／India／Australia

❷ **Padparadscha Sapphire**
Sri Lanka／Madagascar

❸ **Orange Sapphire**
Tanzania／Madagascar／
Sri Lanka

❹ **Pink Sapphire**
Madagascar／Tanzania／
Sri Lanka／Vietnam

❺ **Yellow Sapphire**
Madagascar／Sri Lanka／
Thailand／Australia

❻ **Green Sapphire**
Madagascar／Tanzania

❼ **Brown Sapphire**
Sri Lanka／Madagascar／
Tanzania／Myanmar

❽ **White Sapphire**
Sri Lanka／Madagascar／
Tanzania／Myanmar

　最高ランクに輝くブルーサファイアのなかでも、最高品質のコーンフラワーブルーはインドのカシミール地方が産出地として有名でした。近年は国境紛争もありほとんど産出されません。ミャンマー産のロイヤルブルーについても、国情が不安定なこともありほとんど産出されず、同国のモゴク鉱山はスターサファイアの産出で知られていましたが、これも激減しています。

　1990年代以降、相次いでサファイア鉱床が発見されたのがマダガスカルです。紫色が強いブルーサファイアが採掘され人気があります。

　スリランカも良質のブルーサファイアの産出で知られますが、その量は減少しています。色がやや薄いものの透明度が高く、輝きが美しいのが

Among the highest-ranked blue sapphires, the finest quality cornflower blue sapphires were historically sourced from the Kashmir region of India. However, due to ongoing border conflicts, their production has almost ceased in recent years. Similarly, Myanmar's royal blue sapphires are now rarely mined due to the country's political instability. The Mogok mines in Myanmar, once renowned for producing star sapphires, have also seen a sharp decline in output.

　　Since the 1990s, Madagascar has emerged as a significant source of sapphires, with deposits discovered in succession.

　　The blue sapphires from Madagascar often have a strong purplish tint, making them popular in the market. Sri Lanka is also known for its high-quality blue sapphires, although production has decreased. Sri Lankan sapphires are character-

## Map of Sapphire-Producing Countries

特徴です。タイのカンチャナブリ鉱山、オーストラリアのインベレル鉱山で産出される石は、母岩の影響で色が黒ずんでいる傾向があります。ほかの産地は南アフリカ、ナミビア、ナイジェリアなど。

ブルーと並ぶ最高評価のパパラチアは、スリランカとマダガスカルでのみ産出されます。同系色のピンクサファイア、オレンジサファイアより格段に価値が高いため、鑑別書での確認が重要です。

ファンシーカラーといってもブルーサファイアと同じコランダムなので、1カ所の鉱山からいろいろな色のサファイアが採掘されるケースもあります。スリランカは古くからファンシーカラーの産出で知られ、なかでもラトゥナプラ鉱山が豊富な産出量を誇っていました。

その後、マダガスカルのイラカカ鉱山を中心に採掘が始まりましたが、かつてのような美しいものは少なくなりました。

ピンクサファイアは、タンザニア、ベトナムなどでも産出され、ベトナム産のなかには「ホットピンク」と形容される濃いピンクでテリが強いピンクサファイアがあり、高く評価されます。

オレンジサファイアはスリランカでの産出が減り、一時期は安定供給していたタンザニアでも産出がストップしています。

イエローサファイアはスリランカ、マダガスカルのほか、タイ、オーストラリアで産出され人気です。しかし色が濃く美しいファンシーサファイアは、全体的に減少傾向で価格は上昇しています。

ized by their slightly lighter color, high transparency, and beautiful brilliance. In contrast, sapphires mined in Thailand's Kanchanaburi region and Australia's Inverell mines tend to produce darker colors influenced by the composition of the host rock. Other sources of sapphires include South Africa, Namibia, and Nigeria.

The padparadscha sapphire, which rivals blue sapphires in terms of top ratings, is only found in Sri Lanka and Madagascar. This variety, valued far more highly than similarly colored pink or orange sapphires, requires verification through gemological certificates due to its rarity and significant worth.

Despite being categorized as fancy-colored sapphires, they share the same mineral composition, corundum, as blue sapphires. Thus, it is not uncommon for a single mine to yield sapphires of various colors. Sri Lanka has long been known for its production of fancy-colored sapphires, with the Ratnapura mines boasting abundant output in the past. However, while mining has expanded to Madagascar's Ilakaka mines, the number of truly beautiful sapphires has declined compared to earlier.

Pink sapphires are also mined in Tanzania and Vietnam, with some Vietnamese sapphires described as "hot pink" due to their deep color and strong luster, making them highly valued.

Meanwhile, orange sapphires have seen a drop in production in Sri Lanka, and mining in Tanzania, which once ensured a stable supply, has ceased altogether.

Yellow sapphires are popular, being produced in Sri Lanka, Madagascar, Thailand, and Australia. However, fancy-colored sapphires with deep, beautiful colors are generally in decline, leading to rising prices in the global market.

(Clockwise from top left)
- WG Pendant_Cab Ruby13.67ct,D1.31ct
- Pt Ring_Star Ruby9.52ct,D2.12ct
- Pt Ring_Ruby4.59ct,D1.05ct
- Pt Ring_Ruby5.26ct,D2.07ct
- Pt Ring_Star Ruby5.96ct,D2.49ct

# Ruby

ルビー

### 燃え盛る炎のような赤い輝き

　まるで情熱をたぎらせているようなルビーの赤い輝きは、はるか遠い時代から人の心を掴んで離しませんでした。ラテン語で赤を意味する「ルベウス」が語源です。

　旧約聖書ではソロモン王が幾度もルビーの名を口にし、赤い色の象徴だったことがうかがわれます。古代のギリシャ、ローマではルビーを「燃える石炭」と呼び、燃え盛る炎のような色を崇めました。インドでは「宝石の王者」を意味するラトナンジュと呼んで珍重されました。

### A Fiery Red Brilliance: Like a Blazing Flame

The vivid red brilliance of rubies, reminiscent of unbridled passion, has captivated humanity for centuries. The name "ruby" originates from the Latin word *rubeus*, meaning red.

In the Old Testament, King Solomon is said to have spoken of rubies repeatedly, highlighting their symbolic association with the color red. In ancient Greece and Rome, rubies were called "burning coals" and admired for their fiery, flame-like colors. In India, they were called *ratnaraj*, meaning "king of gemstones," and were highly revered.

# Ruby

ルビー

## 最高評価を受けるピジョンブラッド

　ルビーは鉱物学上はサファイアと同じコランダムです。酸化アルミニウムによりコランダムが形成される際、クロムが１％程度入り込むことで、奇跡のように美しい赤いルビーが生まれます。

　ルビーのなかでも頂点に輝くのが、ピジョンブラッドと呼ばれる色。濃い赤のなかにも柔らかみを感じさせ、鳩の血を思わせるとして、こう形容されます。ミャンマーで産出され、旧国名からビルマルビーとも呼ばれます。加熱処理されたものが多く、非加熱のビルマルビーは非常に高価です。

　一方、タイ産のルビーはやや黒みがかった赤い色が特徴で、牛の血の色にたとえてビーフブラッドと呼ばれます。良く輝きますが、色の面でビルマルビーより評価が下がります。

## Pigeon Blood: The Highest-Rated Ruby

Ruby, like sapphire, is mineralogically corundum composed of aluminum oxide. When about 1% chromium is incorporated into its crystal structure, it creates a stunning red color.

　Among rubies, the pinnacle is the color known as "Pigeon Blood." This term refers to a deep red color with a certain softness, reminiscent of the color of pigeon's blood. These rubies are mined in Myanmar and are also called "Burmese rubies" after the country's former name. While many Burmese rubies undergo heat treatment, untreated ones are extremely rare and highly valuable.

　On the other hand, Thai rubies are characterized by a slightly darker red with a blackish tint. This color is often compared to ox blood, earning them the nickname "Beef Blood." While Thai rubies exhibit intense brilliance, their color is considered less desirable than that of Burmese rubies.

(Clockwise from top)
- Pt Ring_Cab Ruby9.71ct,D2.26ct
- Pt Ring_Ruby1.37ct,D0.72ct
- Pt Ring_Ruby2.31ct,D0.59ct
- YG Ring_Ruby3.90ct,D2.44ct
- Pt Ring_Cab Ruby1.55ct,D0.39ct

(Clockwise from top)
・Pt Pendant_Star Ruby1.64ct,D2.26ct
・Pt Ring_Star Ruby2.22ct,D0.57ct
・Pt Ring_Star Ruby6.651ct,D1.97ct
・Pt Ring_Star Ruby5.16ct,D0.43ct

# Star Ruby

スタールビー

## 大自然の奇跡が生む六条の線

　カボションカットにすると六条の線があらわれるルビーが、スタールビーです。石の中にルチルという物質が内包物として針状に入り込み、星のように見えるアステリズム効果、広くスター効果と呼ばれるものが生まれます。

　スタールビーについてもミャンマー産が多くを占めます。ウランが採れる鉱山で産出されることから、ウランの影響により独特のテリが出るといわれています。ただし、ビルマルビーはファセットカットにしたほうが世界市場で高値がつくため、カボションにすることは減っています。

　そもそも悠久の歴史のなかで奇跡が重なって誕生しただけに、非常にレアな存在。大粒で良質のスタールビーはほとんど市場に出回りません。

## The Six-Rayed Lines Born of Miracles

A ruby that displays six-rayed lines when cut into a cabochon shape is called a star ruby. This phenomenon, known as asterism or, more commonly as the star effect, occurs when needle-like inclusions of a mineral called rutile are present within the stone, creating a star-like appearance.

　The majority of star rubies are sourced from Myanmar. It is said that the unique luster of these rubies may be influenced by uranium, as they are mined in areas where uranium is found. However, because faceted Burmese rubies fetch higher prices on the global market, the practice of cutting them into cabochons has decreased.

　Star rubies are incredibly rare, having been formed through countless natural miracles throughout history. Large, high-quality star rubies are especially scarce and are seldom seen on the market.

# Ruby
## Production Trends and Value

ルビーの産出動向とその価値

ルビーは地層の影響などにより、産出国ごとに特徴と評価が異なります。最高評価のピジョンブラッドを産出するミャンマーでは、モゴク鉱山、マンシュー鉱山で良質の石が採れることが知られています。モゴク鉱山では少量ながら色が濃く鮮やかなスタールビーも産出されます。

やや黒みがかった赤色のルビーが採れるタイでは、近年になり鉱山が閉鎖され、透明度が高く美しいものは値上がりしています。

スリランカのラトゥナプラ鉱山では、明るい赤のルビーが採れます。チェリーピンクと形容されるほど淡い色のものもあり、それだけ評価は下がります。スタールビーも産出され、くっきりした六条の線ながら、やはり色が薄いのが特徴です。

ベトナムで産出されるルビーは、透明度が高く、輝きに優れています。近年は産出が激減し、ほとんど採れなくなりました。

**Map of Ruby-Producing Countries**

※おもな産出国や地域を記載しています
※Main producing countries and regions

このように従来の産出地は東南アジアが中心でしたが、現在はアフリカでも良質のルビーが産出されています。モザンビーク、タンザニア、ケニア、マダガスカルが主な産出国です。

Rubies exhibit unique characteristics and varying evaluations depending on the country of origin, influenced by factors such as geological conditions. Myanmar, known for producing the highest-rated Pigeon Blood rubies, yields high-quality stones from the Mogok and Mansin mines. The Mogok mine also produces a small quantity of star rubies, notable for their vivid and deep coloration.

In Thailand, mines that once produced slightly darker, blackish-red rubies have recently closed, leading to the rising value of high-clarity, exceptionally beautiful rubies.

The Ratnapura mine in Sri Lanka produces rubies with a light red color. Some stones exhibit an even lighter color, often described as "cherry pink," which results in lower evaluations. Star rubies are also found in Sri Lanka, characterized by distinct six-rayed lines, although their color tends to be lighter.

Rubies mined in Vietnam are noted for their high clarity and exceptional brilliance. However, their production has sharply declined recently, with very few being mined today.

While Southeast Asia has traditionally been the primary region for ruby production, high-quality rubies are now mined in Africa. Mozambique, Tanzania, Kenya, and Madagascar have emerged as notable sources of ruby production.

# Ruby & Star Ruby Color Grading Table

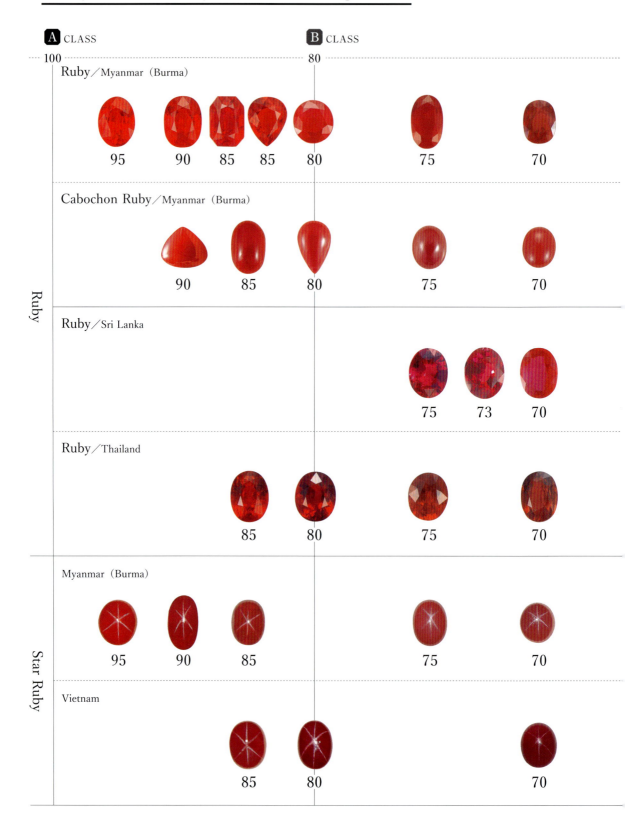

# Ruby

● ルビー　Ruby

チェックポイントは、色、内包物、輝きの3点（p.160参照）。色は濃くなればなるほど点数が高くなる一方で、最高の色を通り越して黒みを帯びると評価が下がります。産出されるルビーの価値とその数はピラミッド同様で、Aクラスの石は全体のごくごく一部であり、Cクラスが最も多い層を占めています。95点のビルマルビーは典型的なピジョンブラッドの逸品。色が暗く、輝きが弱くなるほど点数が下がります。カボションのビルマルビーの90点の石は、内側から燃え立つような赤とテリの良さが印象的。色が浅く、テリと透明感が落ちるほど評価が下がります。スリランカ産のルビーは愛らしいピンクですが、ルビーとしては赤い色が薄いことがわかります。タイ産の85点の石はビーフブラッドの一級品です。黒みを帯びていても透明感とテリが美しい石は高く評価されます。

The three key evaluation points for rubies are color, inclusions, and brilliance(see p.160). The deeper the color, the higher the score; however, the evaluation decreases if the color becomes overly dark and takes on a blackish color. The value and quantity of rubies produced resemble a pyramid: A-class stones account for only a tiny fraction of the total, while C-class stones comprise the largest proportion.A 95-point Burmese ruby is a prime example of a classic Pigeon Blood stone. As the color darkens and brilliance diminishes, the score decreases accordingly. A 90-point cabochon-cut Burmese ruby is impressive for its fiery red color and strong luster. However, as the color lightens and luster and transparency weaken, the evaluation score drops.Rubies from Sri Lanka exhibit a charming pink color, though their red color is considered too light to qualify as top-grade rubies.An 85-point ruby from Thailand is a first-grade Beef Blood stone. Even with a blackish tint, rubies with strong transparency and luster are highly valued.

● スタールビー　Star Ruby

色と六条の線がチェックポイントです。色が美しく、線がはっきりと浮かび上がるほど高く評価されます。カボションの中央できれいに線が交差していることもポイントです。スタールビーは稀少性が非常に高いため、内包物や面キズにはあまり神経質になりすぎなくていいでしょう。ミャンマー産の95点のスタールビーは、濃い赤地にシャープに線が入った最高級品。Aクラスの石は色も線も輝きも美しいことが一目瞭然です。ベトナム産のスタールビーも同様に、色みや透明感によって評価が変わります。

Color and the six-rayed lines are the key evaluation points. The more vivid the color and the clearer the lines, the higher the rating. Another important factor is the neat intersection of the lines at the center of the cabochon. Due to the extreme rarity of star rubies, inclusions and surface blemishes are generally not given too much consideration.A 95-point star ruby from Myanmar is a top-grade gem, featuring a deep red base with sharp, well-defined lines. A-class stones are immediately recognizable for their exceptional color, lines, and brilliance.Similarly, the evaluation of star rubies from Vietnam varies based on their color and transparency.

(From left to right)
- Pt Ring_Emerald4.68ct,D1.62ct
- Pt Pendant_Emerald5.09ct,D1.459ct
- Pt Ring_Emerald2.43ct,D1.50ct
- Pt Ring_Emerald2.74ct,D1.80ct
- Pt Ring_Cab Emerald5.75ct,D1.91ct

# Emerald

エメラルド

### 稀代の権力者に愛された崇高な色石

　得も言われぬ深い緑色が魅惑的なエメラルド。ペルシャ語で緑をあらわす言葉が語源です。「聖なる石」として崇敬され、旧約聖書には神と人間のつながりを象徴する存在として描かれています。

　稀代の権力者がエメラルドにさらなる力を求めたことも知られています。クレオパトラはエメラルド鉱山を所有し、採掘された美しい石に囲まれ、政治の駆け引きにも巧みに用いました。アレキサンダー大王は遠征に際し、勝利を祈念し、大粒のエメラルドを携行したと伝えられます。

### A Sublime Gemstone Cherished by Kings

The mesmerizing deep green of emeralds is truly captivating. The word "emerald" originates from a Persian term meaning "green." Revered as a "sacred stone," emeralds are depicted in the Old Testament as symbols of the connection between God and humanity.

It is well known that kings sought additional power through emeralds. Cleopatra owned emerald mines and surrounded herself with these exquisite gems, skillfully using them in her political maneuvers. Alexander the Great is said to have carried a large emerald during his military campaigns, praying for victory and divine favor.

# Emerald

エメラルド

*(From left to right)*
- Pt Ring_Emerald0.72ct,D0.86ct
- Pt Ring_Emerald1.21ct,D1.00ct
- Pt Ring_Emerald0.62ct,D0.42ct
- WG/YG Pendant_Emerald1.49ct,D0.77ct
- Pt Ring_Emerald1.13ct,D0.59ct

## 産地の母岩により生まれる色みの違い

　エメラルドは鉱物学上はベリル（緑柱石）に属します。アクアマリンやモルガナイトも同じベリルですが、石を構成する微量の酸化クロムや酸素の原子の距離、結晶構造などにより深い緑のエメラルドが生み出されます。

　緑の色合いは、産出地ごとに特徴があります。原石が付着する母岩によって含有される金属元素の量などが異なり、影響を受けるためです。

　エメラルドのなかでも世界一、稀少価値の高い最高級品を産出するのが、南米コロンビア。母岩が白い石灰岩であるため、内包物が入り込んでも黒ずむことなく、澄んだ明るい緑色です。

　同じ南米でもブラジル産は母岩が黒っぽい色で、黒みを帯びたエメラルドが多くなっています。

## Color Variations Shaped by the Host Rock of the Mining Region

Emeralds belong to the mineral family of beryl. Aquamarine and morganite are also varieties of beryl, but the deep green color of emeralds is the result of trace amounts of chromium oxide, the spacing of oxygen atoms, and their crystal structure.

The shade of green varies depending on the country of origin. This is influenced by differences in the metallic elements present in the host rock where the rough crystals form.

Colombia, in South America, is renowned for producing the world's finest and rarest emeralds. The host rock in this region is white limestone, which allows the emeralds to retain a clear, bright green color even when inclusions are present, without appearing dark.

In contrast, emeralds from Brazil, another South American producer, tend to exhibit a darker green color due to the blackish color of the host rock.

# Red Emerald

レッドエメラルド

- Red Emerald 0.449ct
- Pt Pendant_Red Emerald 0.41ct, D0.21ct

## 奇跡が生んだ赤い輝き

エメラルドは緑という常識を覆す存在がレッドエメラルド。酸化クロムの代わりにマンガンが入り込み、赤い色が生まれます。1958年にアメリカ・ユタ州のワーワー山脈で鉱脈が見つかり、「奇跡の赤」として注目されました。1997年から本格的な採掘が始まりましたが、新世紀を迎えると産出はストップ。早くも幻のエメラルドとなりました。

## A Red Brilliance Born of Miracles

Challenging the conventional notion that emeralds are green, red emeralds stand out as a remarkable exception. Instead of chromium oxide, manganese is incorporated, giving these gems their striking red color. In 1958, a vein of red emeralds was discovered in the Wah Wah Mountains of Utah, USA, earning the nickname "Miracle Red." Full-scale mining began in 1997, but as the new century dawned, production ceased, transforming red emeralds into a rare and almost mythical gemstone.

## 緑色に猫の目が浮かぶ不可思議

カボションカットにしたエメラルドに光を当てると一条の線が浮かび、猫の目を思わせるものをエメラルドキャッツアイと呼びます。コロンビア、ザンビア、ブラジルなどで産出されますが、きわめてレアなコレクターズアイテムです。トラピッチェエメラルドは、六方向に花が開くように結晶が伸び、こちらも非常にレアです。

## The Mysterious Phenomenon of a Green Gemstone Revealing a Cat's Eye

When light shines on an emerald cut into a cabochon, a single line resembling a cat's eye may appear. Such stones are known as emerald cat's eyes.

Emerald cat's eyes are found in countries such as Colombia, Zambia, and Brazil, but they are extremely rare and highly prized by collectors. Trapiche emeralds, characterized by a crystal structure that radiates outward in six directions like a blooming flower, are also exceptionally rare.

# Emerald Cat's Eye & Trapiche Emerald

エメラルドキャッツアイ&トラピッチェエメラルド

(From left to right)
- Emerald Cat's Eye 0.34ct
- Emerald Cat's Eye 2.01ct
- Emerald Cat's Eye 0.44ct

(Clockwise from the top)
- Trapiche Emerald 0.90ct
- Trapiche Emerald 1.75ct
- Trapiche Emerald 0.78ct
- Trapiche Emerald 0.82ct

# Emerald
## Production Trends and Value
エメラルドの産出動向とその価値

エメラルドの産地として世界的に名高いのが南米のコロンビア。アンデス山脈のムゾー鉱山のほかチボール鉱山、ピタ鉱山などが知られています。かつてはコロンビア産が全エメラルドの8割を占めましたが、産出量が激減し、品薄により高騰しました。近年は国内情勢が混乱を極めた頃と比べると落ち着き、流通の整備が進んで闇取引がほぼなくなりましたが、高止まりしています。

ブラジル産は黒ずんでいる特徴があり、質の高い石が安定して採れる状況ではありません。

アフリカでエメラルド産出国として知られるのがザンビアです。母岩が黒いことから黒みを帯びた石が多い傾向がありますが、近年は透明感のあるものも産出されています。カボションカットにすることも多くあります。

エチオピア、ソマリア、ジンバブエ、南アフリカ、またマダガスカルでも、エメラルドは産出されます。最高の色みとはいえない品質の石が多いものの、なかにはコロンビア産にひけをとらない美しい色の石もあります。ただし、産出量が非常に少なく、ほとんど採れていません。

Colombia in South America is renowned worldwide as a premier producer of emeralds. Mines in the Andes Mountains, such as the Muzo, Chivor, and La Pita mines, are particularly well-known. At one point, Colombian emeralds accounted for 80% of the global supply. However, production has significantly declined, resulting in shortages and steep price increases. In recent years, the country has become more stable compared to its period of severe domestic turmoil, with improved distribution networks that have nearly eradicated black market transactions. Nevertheless, prices remain high.

Emeralds from Brazil are known for their darker, blackish color, but consistent production of high-quality stones remains a challenge.

In Africa, Zambia is a notable emerald producer. Due to the dark host rock, many Zambian emeralds have a blackish tone. However, in recent years, more transparent stones have also been mined. These emeralds are often cut into cabochons.

Emeralds are also mined in Ethiopia, Somalia, Zimbabwe, South Africa, and Madagascar. While many of these stones lack the ideal coloration, some exhibit stunning colors that rival Colombian emeralds. However, the production volume is extremely limited, and only a small quantity meets the highest standards.

# Emerald Color Grading Table

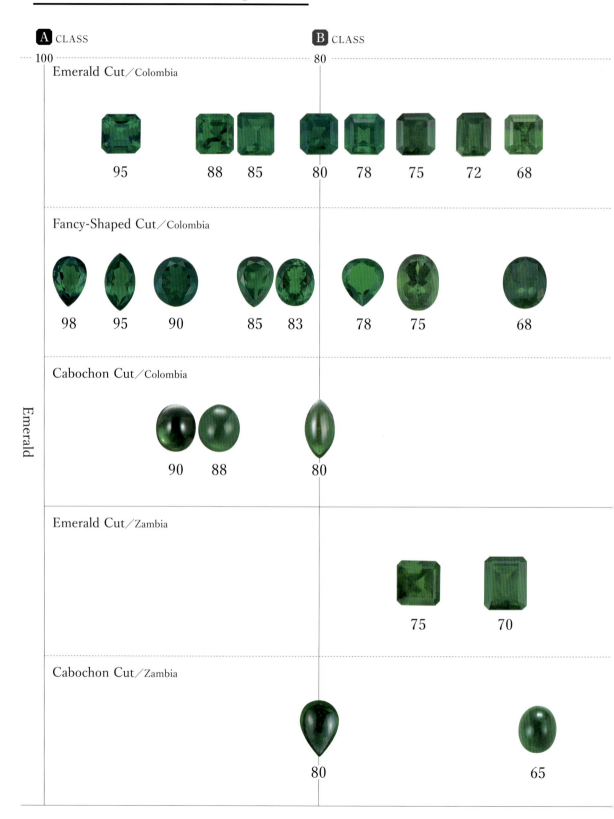

# Emerald

## C CLASS

Untreated Russian Emeralds: Unique Luster, Striking Color, and Exceptional Rarity
加熱処理されていないロシア産エメラルド。独特のテリがあって美しい。非常に稀少。

評価基準となるのは、色、内包物、輝きの3点。特に重視されるのが色であり、緑の色が濃くなればなるほど高い得点がつけられます。ただし、最高の色合いを通り越し、黒ずんだ緑色に見えると減点されます。エメラルドは内包物の多い宝石です。入り込んでいるのは主に酸化クロムで、これが美しい緑の源でもあります。石の中央などにあって美しさを損なわない限り、あまりとらわれる必要はありません。輝きについては、表面がくもっている印象を受ける石は評価が低くなります。光を受けて、深い海の中のように輝くものが高い点数を獲得します。

The evaluation criteria for emeralds consist of three key aspects: color, inclusions, and brilliance. Among these, color is the most important factor—the deeper and richer the green color, the higher the score. However, if the color becomes excessively dark and takes on a blackish color, points are deducted. Emeralds are known as gemstones rich in inclusions. These inclusions are primarily chromium oxide, which also contributes to their vivid green color. As long as the inclusions are not positioned in a way that significantly detracts from the gemstone's beauty—such as being prominently located in the center—they are not a major concern. As for brilliance, emeralds with a cloudy or dull surface are rated lower. Stones that radiate a glow reminiscent of the depths of the ocean receive higher scores.

● コロンビア産　Colombia

95点のエメラルドカットは、エメラルドグリーンの美しさを体現している逸品です。透明感もテリも文句のつけようがない石です。72点と65点はキズがマイナスポイント。色が浅いものはCクラスに位置づけられます。ファンシーシェイプカットでもAクラスの石は、色み、透明感、独特のテリが際立っているのがわかります。カボションカットの90点は、半透明の色みとテリが美しい一級品。カボションカットはエメラルドカットと比べると価格が割安ではありますが、エメラルドはいずれも全般的に値上がりしています。

A 95-point emerald-cut piece is a masterpiece that perfectly embodies the beauty of emerald green. Its transparency and luster are flawless, leaving nothing to be desired. In contrast, 72-point and 65-point stones lose points due to visible flaws. Stones with lighter colors are categorized as C-class. A-class stones are also distinguished in fancy-shaped cuts by their exceptional color, transparency, and unique luster. A 90-point cabochon-cut emerald, with its semi-transparent color and beautiful luster, is a top-grade gem. While cabochon-cut emeralds are generally more affordable than faceted emeralds, emerald prices overall have been steadily rising.

● ザンビア産　Zambia

エメラルドカット、カボションカットともに、コロンビア産よりも黒みが強いことがわかります。色の深み、テリ、透明度、キズの有無などにより評価が変わります。

Both emerald-cut and cabochon-cut emeralds tend to display a stronger blackish tone compared to those from Colombia. Their evaluation depends on factors such as color depth, luster, transparency, and the presence or absence of flaws.

(From top left to right)
- Pt Ring_Alexandrite1.20ct,D1.75ct
- Alexandrite4.05ct
- Pt Pendant_Alexandrite4.48ct,D1.89ct
- Pt Ring_Alexandrite1.10ct,D0.82ct

# Alexandrite

アレキサンドライト

## 魔法のように変色する「宝石の王様」

　アレキサンドライトの最大の特徴は、当たる光により色が変わる変色性。アレキサンドライトのほか、ごく一部の石だけが有する類い稀な性質です。自然光のもとではグリーンに輝き、白熱灯では赤く輝く変身ぶりに、見る人は心を奪われます。

　発見されたのは1830年、ロシアのウラル山脈にあるエメラルド鉱山でのこと。ロマノフ王朝の皇太子アレクサンドル2世の誕生日だったことから、アレキサンドライトと名付けられました。歴史が短いながら「宝石の王様」と称えられます。

## The 'King of Gemstones' That Magically Changes Color

The most distinctive feature of alexandrite is its extraordinary ability to change color, a rare phenomenon found in only a few gemstones. Under natural light, it glows green, while under incandescent light, it transforms into a vibrant red. This dramatic color shift captivates all who behold it.

　Alexandrite was discovered in 1830 at an emerald mine in Russia's Ural Mountains. It was named after Tsarevich Alexander II of the Romanov dynasty, as the discovery coincided with his birthday. Despite its relatively short history, alexandrite is revered as the "King of Gemstones."

Alexandrite

(From top left to right)
- Pt Ring_Alexandrite1.70ct,D0.58ct
- Pt Ring_Alexandrite0.60ct,D0.43ct

(Middle row left to right)
- Pt Ring_Alexandrite1.16ct,D0.44ct
- Pt Ring_Alexandrite5.30ct,D2.16ct
- Pt Ring_Alexandrite1.44ct,D1.66ct

(Bottom)
- Pt Ring_Alexandrite1.08ct,D1.31ct

# Alexandrite

アレキサンドライト

## 赤から緑へと変わる自然の驚異

　アレキサンドライトは鉱物学上はキャッツアイなどと同じクリソベリルに属します。2色に変わる理由は、内包物として入り込んでいる酸化クロムにあります。光の種類によって緑、赤のいずれかの特徴が強く出るという自然の驚異です。

　さまざまな研究が進み、アレキサンドライトは地上で生まれた最古の宝石と判明しました。19世紀になり発見され、40億年以上の眠りから覚めて人々に愛でられることになりました。

　特に高い価値を見出されるのは、はっきりと変色する石ですが、現実的には、一方の色がきれいに出ると、もう一方の色は鮮やかにならない石がほとんどです。それでも、いずれかの色が鮮明で美しい色合いであれば、高く評価されます。

　どのような色に変色するかによっても価値は大きく変わります。理想は深い赤紫からエメラルドのような緑や青緑に変色するものですが、そのような石は幻の逸品。ほとんどは茶色がかった赤と青み、黄みを帯びた緑色です。良質の石の価格は非常に高騰しています。

(From top to bottom)
- Pt Ring_Alexandrite0.84ct,D0.55ct
- Pt Ring_Alexandrite0.678ct,D0.34ct
- Pt Ring_Alexandrite4.81ct,D1.52ct
- Alexandrite2.48ct

## A Natural Marvel That Changes from Red to Green

Mineralogically, alexandrite belongs to the chrysoberyl family, alongside cat's eye. The reason for its color change lies in the presence of chromium oxide as inclusions. Depending on the type of light, either green or red colors become more pronounced—a true marvel of nature.

　Research has shown that alexandrite is one of the oldest gemstones formed on Earth. Discovered in the 19th century, it emerged from a slumber of more than 4 billion years to enchant humanity.

　Stones that exhibit a distinct and dramatic color change are particularly prized. However, in most cases, when one color appears vividly, the other is less vibrant. Even so, alexandrite is highly valued if either color is vivid and displays a beautiful tone.

　The value of alexandrite also depends significantly on the specific colors it changes to. The ideal transition is from a deep reddish-purple to an emerald-like green or bluish-green. Such stones, however, are exceedingly rare and considered legendary. Most alexandrites, however, display a brownish-red and a green with bluish or yellowish tones. The price of high-quality alexandrite has surged dramatically in recent years.

# Alexandrite
## Production Trends and Value

アレキサンドライトの産出動向とその価値

アレキサンドライトは産出地により異なる特徴を有します。

はじめに発見されたロシアのウラル山脈ではほとんど産出されなくなり、代わって世界のアレキサンドライト産出の中心となったのがブラジルです。ヘマチタ鉱山で赤茶色から青緑色に変色する石が採れます。美しい赤紫色から青緑色へ変化する良質なものがありますが、一級品は限られます。そのうえ、Aランクに届かないBランクの石の産出も減り、価格は上昇する一方です。

ほかに、スリランカ、アフリカなどで質の高い石が産出されてきました。

スリランカ産は、濃い赤茶色から緑色へと変色するのが特徴。この色みによりブラジル産の良質のアレキサンドライトと比べると、ワンランク下がります。ただし、小粒が多いブラジル産とは対照的に大粒のものも見られます。

タンザニア、マダガスカル、さらにインドで産出されるものは、ブラジル産とスリランカ産のちょうど中間の色合いです。

Alexandrite exhibits distinct characteristics depending on its country of origin.

In the Ural Mountains of Russia, where alexandrite was first discovered, production has significantly declined. Brazil has since become the world's leading source of alexandrite. At the Hematita mine in Brazil, stones that change color from reddish-brown to bluish-green are found. Some high-quality specimens display a transition from a vivid reddish-purple to bluish-green, but top-grade stones are extremely rare. Additionally, the production of B-grade stones, which do not meet A-grade standards, has also declined, causing prices to rise steadily.

High-quality alexandrite has also been mined in Sri Lanka and parts of Africa.

Sri Lankan alexandrites are known for their color change from deep reddish-brown to green. However, this color profile places them one tier below the high-quality Brazilian alexandrites. That said, Sri Lankan stones are often larger in size compared to the predominantly smaller Brazilian stones.

Alexandrites from Tanzania, Madagascar, and India exhibit a color profile that falls between those of Brazilian and Sri Lankan stones.

# Alexandrite Color Grading Table

# Alexandrite

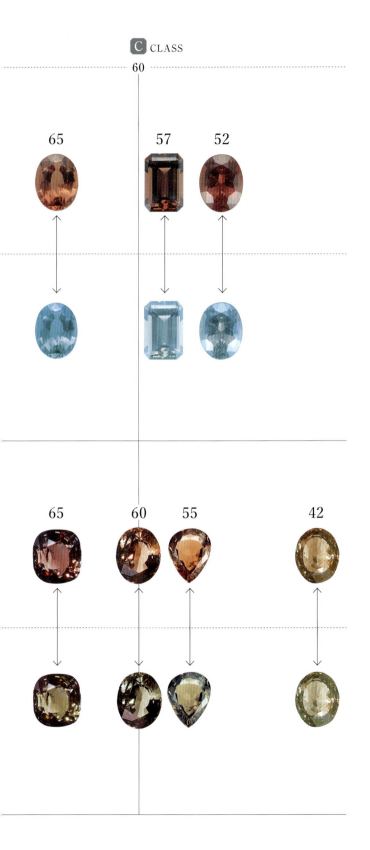

色の変化が明らかで色みが美しいアレキサンドライトには、大変高い価値があります。変色性の度合いが明確であるほど高得点となり、赤から緑へはっきりと色を変えることが重要です。反対に、色が変わる度合いが低い石は評価が下がります。購入する際は鑑別書に記された色相の変化をしっかりと確認し、自分自身の目でも確かめるように気をつけましょう。ほかの色石と同じく、色は濃くなればなるほど評価は高くなります。ただし、深い赤紫からエメラルドのような深い緑色に変わる石は現実にはほとんどありません。茶色がかった赤、青みの強い緑がアレキサンドライトの色合いの特徴といえます。また、赤がきれいな場合は緑が弱かったり、緑が鮮やかでも赤は弱かったりするので、いずれかの色合いがしっかりと出ていることも評価のポイントです。変色性と色合いに加えて、内包物と輝きを評価します。

Alexandrite with a clear and vivid color change holds exceptionally high value. The more distinct and dramatic the degree of color change, the higher the score. A sharp transition from red to green is particularly important. Conversely, stones with a less noticeable color change are rated lower. When purchasing alexandrite, it is essential to carefully review the description of the color change on the gemological certificate and confirm it with your own eyes. As with other colored gemstones, deeper colors are generally more highly valued. However, in reality, stones that transition from deep reddish-purple to deep emerald-like green are exceedingly rare. Most alexandrites display a brownish-red color and green with strong blue tones. Moreover, when the red color is vivid, the green may appear weaker, and vice versa. For this reason, the clarity and beauty of either color are crucial evaluation factors. In addition to color change and color quality, inclusions and brilliance are also taken into account during the evaluation process.

● ブラジル産　Brazil

Aクラスの石は、赤紫色から青緑色への変色が実に見事です。色みも輝きも美しく、それこそがアレキサンドライトの魅力です。点数が下がるとともに、深みある色の美しさ、透明感のある輝きが薄らいでいきます。

A-class alexandrite displays an extraordinary color change from reddish-purple to bluish-green. Its colors and brilliance are breathtaking, perfectly embodying the allure of alexandrite. However, as the grading score decreases, the richness of color, its beauty, and the transparency of the brilliance gradually fade.

● スリランカ産、タンザニア産
　Sri Lanka, Tanzania

赤茶色から緑色への変色が特徴的です。Aクラスの2つはタンザニア産。90点の石は鮮烈な赤と緑で、ほとんど出合うことがない逸品です。70点以下はスリランカ産の石であり、色みが違います。BクラスからCクラスへといくほど、変色の度合いが低くなることがわかります。

A distinctive feature of these stones is their color change from reddish-brown to green. The two A-class stones are from Tanzania. The 90-point stone, with its vivid red and green colors, is an exceptionally rare masterpiece. Stones scoring 70 points or below are from Sri Lanka and exhibit different color tones. As the grading decreases from B-class to C-class, the degree of color change becomes noticeably weaker.

097

# 世界的に色石への興味が飛躍的に高まっています

**Global Interest in Colored Gemstones Is Rising Significantly**

## 投資熱に沸く世界の色石市場

　宝石商は祖父の代からの家業です。祖父と父はインドのジャイプールで仕事をしていましたが、私は海外に出て日本、アメリカ、香港と拠点を移し、数年前からドバイに腰を落ち着けました。さまざまな色石を扱っていますが、なかでも稀少石のパライバトルマリンやアレキサンドライト、それにスピネルを中心に扱っています。

　現在、世界の宝石市場の中心といえば日本、アメリカ、中国。最も多くの種類の石が集まるのが日本でしょう。日本ではレアな宝石、ユニークな宝石全般の人気があり、エメラルドやサファイアなどに人気が集中するアメリカとは対照的です。ブラジルでパライバトルマリンが発見されたとき

### The Global Colored Gemstone Market: A Hotbed of Investment Frenzy

I come from a family of gem traders, a business that has been passed down since my grandfather's time. While my grandfather and father worked in Jaipur, India, I expanded internationally, setting up bases in Japan, the United States, and Hong Kong before settling in Dubai a few years ago. I deal in a variety of colored gemstones, with a particular focus on rare stones such as Paraiba tourmaline, alexandrite, and spinel.

Today, the global gemstone market is centered around Japan, the United States, and China. Among them, Japan stands out as the country where the widest variety of gemstones converge. Japanese

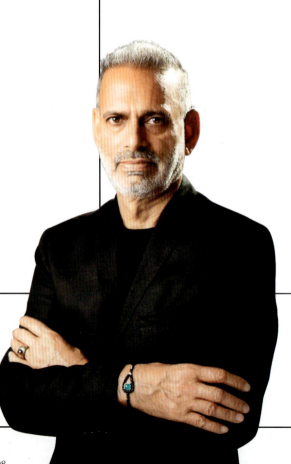

## Interview

ドバイの宝石ディーラー
# ザヒール・アンサリ氏

**Dubai Gem Dealer:
Mr. Zaheer Ansari**

も、はじめに購入したのは日本人だけ。それからほかの国に人気が広がり、今日まで上昇が続いています。

以前と比べて、色石への関心は世界的に高まりました。身に着けるためだけでなく、投資として捉え、購入する人が格段に増えています。

中東の色石市場については、まだ新しく、どんどん変化するのを目の当たりにしています。私が8年程前にドバイに来たころ、色石や稀少石は、ほとんど知られていませんでした。今では認知度が大きく上がり、理解が深まっています。

アレキサンドライトへの投資熱も相当なものです。ロシア、ブラジル、スリランカ、アフリカ、インドの鉱山のどこもほぼ採り尽くし、値上がりが続いています。投資用に大きな石を探す人が多く、「すべて見せて」「すべて欲しい」と10～15カラットの石3つを現金で購入した顧客もいました。驚いたことに、彼は2カ月後に「もっと欲しい」と、さらに2つ買ったのです。特に色石に詳しいわけではなく、値上がりを聞きつけての購入でした。

ほかの稀少石も軒並み値上がりしています。いずれも産出が減り、市場に流通している石は多くありません。新しい鉱山が見つからない限り、値段は上がり続けるでしょう。購入するなら今日にでも買ったほうがいいですね。近年の国際情勢の不安定さも需要に拍車をかけています。万一のとき、宝石なら簡単に懐に入れて持ち出せますから。大きな石を求める問い合わせも増えています。

consumers have a strong interest in rare and unique gems, in contrast to the U.S., where demand is more focused on emeralds and sapphires. When Paraiba tourmaline was first discovered in Brazil, Japanese buyers were the first to purchase it. Only afterward did interest spread globally, and its value has continued to rise ever since.

Compared to the past, global interest in colored gemstones has grown significantly. More people are now buying them not only for personal adornment but also as investment assets.

The Middle Eastern colored gemstone market is still young, and I have witnessed its rapid transformation firsthand. When I arrived in Dubai about eight years ago, colored and rare gemstones were largely unknown in the region. Today, awareness has increased significantly, and appreciation for these stones continues to grow.

Investment demand for alexandrite is particularly strong. Mines in Russia, Brazil, Sri Lanka, Africa, and India are nearly depleted, pushing prices steadily upward. Many investors are searching for large stones, and I once had a client purchase three alexandrites of 10 to 15 carats each in cash, saying, "Show me everything you have, and I'll take it all." To my surprise, he returned two months later, asking for more and buying two additional stones. He was not particularly knowledgeable about colored gemstones but was drawn to them purely as an investment after hearing about their rising value.

Other rare gemstones are also seeing price surges due to decreasing supply. Very few are circulating in the market, and unless new mines are discovered, prices will only continue to climb. If

## Profile

ヌールジェムジャパン株式会社　代表取締役
NOOR GEMS JAPAN CO., LTD　President

### 宝石のエネルギーや魅力を世に広めたい

パライバトルマリンとアレキサンドライトは、宝石のなかでもエネルギーが特に強い石だと私は感じています。私の会社がここまで発展したのも、非常に美しいうえ、ずば抜けて強いエネルギーのあるパライバと出会い、取り扱えるようになったおかげです。

私にさまざまな色石の知識や宝石のエネルギーを教えてくれたのは、ギンザベルエトワールの前代表の岡本憲将さんでした。今から15年ほど前、ビジネスの不振に苦しむ私に岡本さんは「君に必要なのはこの石だ。これを身につけなさい」とキャッツアイを差し出してくれました。その指輪をつけてから、ビジネスも私自身の調子も急にすべてが上向きになったのです。それ以来私は宝石のエネルギーを実感するようになりました。同じように宝石で人生が好転した人を、たくさん知っています。

岡本さんの特別な思い出として、アメリカの

## ドバイに夢だった宝石ミュージアムをオープン

### Fulfilling a Dream: Opening a Gem Museum in Dubai

世界中のレアストーンが展示されるドバイの宝石ミュージアム

Dubai's gemstone museum, showcasing rare stones from around the world

**Interview** Mr. Zaheer Ansari

GIA（米国宝石学会）本部での講演があります。宝石がもつエネルギーについて、GIAで学ぶ人たちにも伝えたいという岡本さんの思いを受けて、私が友人を介してGIAに掛け合い実現しました。

講演の中で岡本さんは、ふたつのグラスにワインを注ぎ、ひとつにはパライバを持って手をかざし、エネルギーを送りました。するとそちらのワインの味が劇的に変化したのです。これには参加した皆さんもびっくり。宝石のエネルギーを体感して、GIAの皆さんもとても喜び、感謝していました。

先日、長年の夢が実現し、ドバイで宝石ミュージアムをオープンしました。色石を展示するだけでなく、産地や価値、価格の変動、そしてエネルギーについて正しく学べる場となるよう今後仲間たちとさまざまなイベントを企画する予定です。宝石のエネルギーについては岡本敬人さんにも講演をお願いする予定です。展示する宝石は40～50種類。パライバをはじめ、世界の色石、稀少石を紹介します。多くの方々に色石の魅力を深く知っていただきたいと心より願っています。

宝石のエネルギーに導かれてここまできたと話すザヒール氏
Mr. Zaheer says the energy of gemstones has guided him on his journey

you are considering a purchase, now is the time.

Additionally, ongoing global uncertainty has further fueled demand. In times of crisis, gemstones offer a highly portable and discreet form of wealth. As a result, inquiries for larger stones have been increasing.

## I Want to Share the Energy and Beauty of Gemstones with the World

Paraiba tourmaline and alexandrite are, in my experience, gemstones with exceptionally strong energy. I believe that my company's growth and success were largely due to encountering Paraiba tourmaline—a gemstone that is not only extraordinarily beautiful but also radiates unparalleled energy.

It was Mr. Kensho Okamoto, the former president of Ginza Belle Etoile, who taught me about colored gemstones and their energy. About 15 years ago, during a time when my business was struggling, Mr. Okamoto handed me a cat's eye gemstone, saying, "This is the stone you need. Wear it." From the moment I started wearing that ring, everything changed—my business improved, and even my personal outlook became more positive. Since then, I have truly experienced the energy of gemstones. I also know many others whose lives have dramatically improved because of them.

One of my most treasured memories with Mr. Okamoto was his lecture at the GIA (Gemological Institute of America) headquarters in the United States. He wanted to share the energy of gemstones with GIA students, so I worked with a friend to arrange the opportunity. During the lecture, he performed a demonstration—he poured wine into two glasses and, while holding a Paraiba tourmaline, directed its energy toward one of them. To everyone's astonishment, the taste of that wine changed significantly. The attendees were amazed to experience gemstone energy firsthand, and the GIA members were deeply moved and expressed their gratitude.

Recently, I achieved a long-time dream by opening a gemstone museum in Dubai. This space is not just for displaying colored gemstones but also serves as a place where people can learn about their origins, value, price trends, and energy. Together with my colleagues, I plan to organize various events, including lectures by Mr. Takahito Okamoto on gemstone energy. The museum will showcase around 40 to 50 types of gemstones, including Paraiba tourmaline and other rare stones from around the world. I sincerely hope more people appreciate the deeper allure of colored gemstones.

(Clockwise from top left)
・Alexandrite Cat's Eye 3.259ct
・Pt Ring_Alexandrite Cat's Eye 2.559ct, D0.04ct
・Pt Ring_Cat's Eye 4.32ct, D1.59ct
・Cat's Eye 24.93ct
・Pt Ring_Cat's Eye 14.95ct, D3.18ct

# Cat's Eye

キャッツアイ

## 心を捉える猫目の妖しい魅力

石の中央に一条の線が浮かび、猫の目のように妖しく輝くキャッツアイ。心をかきたてる美しさを見れば、古来、人々が特別な力が宿ると信じてきたことに大いに納得がいくでしょう。石に魔神が棲みつき、身につけていれば災難から守ってくれると信じられていたともいいます。

古代のアッシリアでは、祈祷を受ける際にキャッツアイをつけていれば、透明人間になれるとの言い伝えまでありました。東洋では広く、金運と幸運を招く石として珍重されています。

## The Enchanting and Bewitching Charm of Cat Eyes

A single line appears at the center of the stone, gleaming mysteriously like a cat's eye. Its evocative beauty stirs the heart and makes it easy to understand why, throughout history, people have believed that cat's eye stones are imbued with special powers. It was even said that a powerful spirit or deity resided within the stone, offering protection from misfortune to those who wore it.

In ancient Assyria, there was even a legend that wearing a cat's eye while receiving prayers could grant the wearer invisibility. In the East, these stones have long been highly valued as symbols of wealth and good fortune.

# Cat's Eye

キャッツアイ

## 黄色、緑、褐色など幅広い色み

　キャッツアイというのは、1種類の宝石をさす言葉ではありません。カボションカットにすると石の上に猫の目のような一条の線が浮かび上がり、石を動かすと線が左右に動く色石の総称です。これはシャトヤンシー効果といわれ、石の内部に入った針状の内包物に光があたって起こります。

　シャトヤンシー効果が見られる色石は、トルマリン、エメラルドなど約50種類にも上ります。一般的に宝石の名称としてキャッツアイという場合は、ここで紹介するクリソベリルキャッツアイをあらわします。光の帯が石の中央に位置し、シャープで鮮明であるほど高い価値があります。

　色合いは黄色、緑から褐色まで幅広く、和名は猫目石。最も高く評価されるのは、ハニーカラーと呼ばれる蜂蜜のようなトロリとした褐色系の黄色と濃い黄緑色のアップルグリーンです。

## A Wide Range of Colors, Including Yellow, Green, and Brown

The term "cat's eye" does not refer to a single type of gemstone. It is a general term for colored gemstones that, when cut into a cabochon, show a single line resembling a cat's eye. This line shifts from side to side as the stone moves. The effect, known as chatoyancy, occurs when light hits needle-like inclusions inside the stone.

　More than 50 types of gemstones, such as tourmaline and emerald, can show this effect. However, the term "cat's eye" as a gemstone name usually refers to chrysoberyl cat's eye, like the one featured here. Stones with a sharp, clear line centered in the stone are the most valuable.

　Cat's eyes come in various colors, including yellow, green, and brown. The most prized colors are a brownish yellow with a honeyed appearance, known as "honey color," and a deep yellow-green called "apple green."

*(Clockwise from top left)*
- *Pt Pendant_Cat's Eye3.49ct,D1.77ct*
- *Pt Ring_Cat's Eye7.46ct,D1.25ct*
- *Pt Ring_Cat's Eye4.15ct,D2.62ct*
- *Pt Ring_Cat's Eye2.20ct,D1.31ct*
- *Pt Ring_Cat's Eye2.94ct,D0.62ct*

(From left to right)
- Pt Ring_Alexandrite Cat's Eye 2.75ct, D0.10ct
- Pt Ring_Alexandrite Cat's Eye 3.59ct, D2.51ct
- Pt Ring_Alexandrite Cat's Eye 1.51ct, D0.71ct

# Alexandrite Cat's Eye

アレキサンドライトキャッツアイ

## 奇跡が重なり誕生した石

　アレキサンドライトは光源の種類によって赤から緑へと色が変わる性質をもつ宝石。一般的なキャッツアイと同じくクリソベリルに属し、やはりキャッツアイ効果のあらわれる石が存在します。

　といっても、鮮やかな変色性のあるアレキサンドライト自体が稀有な存在です。そこにシャトヤンシー効果が重なるのは、まさに天文学的な確率の出来事といえます。猫の目のように一条の線が浮かび、なおかつはっきりと色が変わるアレキサンドライトキャッツアイにお目にかかれる機会は、大変少ないでしょう。

　良質なアレキサンドライトキャッツアイが産出される量はごくわずかで、市場に流通することも少なく、コレクターズアイテムといえます。

## A Stone Born from a Series of Miracles

Alexandrite is a gemstone that changes color from red to green depending on the light source. Like general cat's eye stones, it belongs to the chrysoberyl family, and some alexandrites also exhibit the cat's eye effect.

However, alexandrite with vivid color-changing properties is already an exceptionally rare gemstone. The combination of this with the chatoyancy effect is an event of astronomical probability. An alexandrite cat's eye, with both a sharp cat's-eye-like line and a clear color change, is something one has very few chances to see.

The production of high-quality alexandrite cat's eye stones is extremely limited, and they rarely appear on the market. These stones are true collector's items.

# Cat's Eye
## Production Trends and Value
### キャッツアイの産出動向とその価値

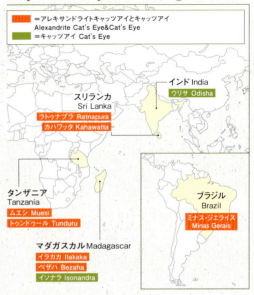

質の高いキャッツアイの産出量は、減少の一途をたどっています。特にハニーカラー、アップルグリーンの大粒は採れなくなり、市場に出回ることは非常に少なくなりました。産出される石の多くは褐色やベージュ系の色みです。

かつては、キャッツアイ、アレキサンドライトキャッツアイとも、スリランカとブラジルが主要産地でした。スリランカでは大粒のハニーカラーの逸品も産出され、線の出方も優れていましたが、すでに激減しています。ブラジルのミナス・ジェライス州では透明度はあるものの線が薄い石がほとんどでしたが、ごく稀にアレキサンドライトキャッツアイの超特級品が採れました。こちらも産出量はゼロに近い状況となっています。

1990年代の終わり頃から採掘が始まったのが、マダガスカルとタンザニアです。マダガスカルでは、スリランカ産と並ぶ良質のキャッツアイがイラカカとその近辺から見つかり、注目されました。アレキサンドライトキャッツアイも産出されました。タンザニアのムエシ、トゥンドゥールでも、キャッツアイ、アレキサンドライトキャッツアイの両方が採れましたが、量が減っています。

インドのウリサ鉱山では稀にアップルグリーンのキャッツアイが採れましたが、現在は薄い黄色で線がぼやけたものがほとんどです。

The production of high-quality cat's eyes has been steadily decreasing. Large stones in honey color or apple green are no longer mined and are now extremely rare in the market. Most of the stones currently being produced are in brown or beige colors.

Sri Lanka and Brazil were once the primary sources of cat's eyes and alexandrite cat's eyes. Sri Lanka produced large honey-colored stones with sharp, well-defined lines, but their production has drastically diminished. In Minas Gerais, while transparent stones were found, most had faint lines. On extremely rare occasions, however, the region yielded exceptional-grade alexandrite cat's eyes. Today, production has nearly ceased.

Mining began in Madagascar and Tanzania at the end of the 1990s. Madagascar gained attention for producing high-quality cat's eyes comparable to those from Sri Lanka, particularly in the Ilakaka region and its surroundings. Alexandrite cat's eyes were also found there. In Tanzania, the Mwezi and Tunduru regions produced both cat's eyes and alexandrite cat's eyes, but output has since declined.

In India's Odisha mines, apple green cat's eyes were sometimes discovered, but today, most stones mined are pale yellow with blurred lines.

# Cat's Eye Color Grading Table

# Cat's Eye

キャッツアイを評価する際に最も重要なポイントは、シャトヤンシー効果がどれほど美しくあらわれているかです。線がシャープに鮮明に出ているほど高評価。線が石の中央に走っていることも大切です。

The most important factor in evaluating a cat's eye gemstone is the beauty of its chatoyancy effect. The sharper and more distinct the line, the higher the evaluation. It is also important that the line runs through the center of the stone.

● キャッツアイ　Cat's Eye

最も高く評価されるのは、アップルグリーンと呼ばれる緑色とハニーカラーと呼ばれる黄褐色の2色。インド産のAクラスの石にアップルグリーンの美しさを見ることができます。スリランカ産、マダガスカル産の90点台の石は、ハニーカラーの逸品。深い蜂蜜色に加え、透明感があり、線がはっきりしています。黒みが強かったり、線がぼやけた印象であったり、内包物が目立ったりすると、マイナスの評価となります。実際に市場に出回っているキャッツアイでハニーカラー、アップルグリーンの石は、わずか1％程度。褐色、ベージュ系などの色合いがほとんどです。

The most highly valued colors of cat's eye stones are two shades: apple green, a green tone, and honey color, a yellow-brown tone. The beauty of apple green can be found in A-class stones from India. Stones from Sri Lanka and Madagascar in the 90-point range are considered exceptional examples of honey color. These stones have a deep honey-like tone, with added transparency and sharp, well-defined lines. On the other hand, stones with a darker tone, blurred lines, or noticeable inclusions receive lower evaluations. Among cat's eye stones currently available on the market, those in honey color or apple green make up only about 1%. Most stones feature shades of brown or beige.

● アレキサンドライトキャッツアイ
　Alexandrite Cat's Eye

大変稀少な存在であるだけに、キャッツアイのなかでもハニーカラー、アップルグリーンのさらに上をいく高い評価を受けます。赤茶と緑の色の変化が鮮明で、いずれも美しい色み、テリがあることに加え、線がクリアである石が、最高評価を受けます。96点の石はブラジル産で、完璧に限りなく近く、奇跡のような最高級品。Bクラス、Cクラスと見比べていくと、色の変わり方があいまいで、線がはっきりせず、途中で途切れていたりすると点数が下がることがわかります。

Due to their extreme rarity, alexandrite cat's eyes receive even higher evaluations than those in honey color and apple green. Stones with a vivid color change between reddish-brown and green, both with beautiful colors and luster, and a sharp, clear line, are given the highest ratings. A 96-point stone from Brazil is an extraordinary, near-perfect masterpiece—a true miracle of nature. In comparison, B-class and C-class stones have less distinct color changes, unclear or interrupted lines, and sometimes incomplete lines, resulting in lower scores.

(From left to right)
- Pt Pendant_Lavender Jade3.49ct.D0.21ct
- Pt Ring_Lavender Jade13.16ct.D0.57ct
- Pt Ring_Jade5.525ct,D2.226ct
- YG Pendant_Jade5.80ct
- Jade4.41ct

# Jade

ヒスイ

### 気品あふれる東洋の財宝

　しっとりと落ち着いた気品ある風情が、ほかの宝石とは一線を画す魅力をもつヒスイ。東洋では護符として、幸運を招く石として古くから深く愛されてきました。漢字の「翡翠」は、実は鳥のカワセミのこと。「空飛ぶ宝石」と形容される鮮やかな羽の美しさから、ヒスイに用いられるようになりました。

　圧倒的に人気があるヒスイは緑で、薄紫色のラベンダーも高く評価されます。ほかにも、あまり評価されないものの、赤、白、黄色、オレンジ、黒などがあります。

### Elegant Treasures of the Orient

Jade, with its serene and refined beauty, possesses a distinctive allure that sets it apart from other gemstones. In Eastern cultures, it has been deeply cherished for centuries as a protective talisman and a stone believed to bring good fortune. Interestingly, the Chinese characters for "jade" (**翡翠**) originally referred to the kingfisher bird. The bird's vibrant plumage, often called "jewels in flight," inspired its connection to jade's exquisite luster.

　Green jade is overwhelmingly popular, while the soft lavender variety is also highly valued. Additionally, jade comes in other colors, such as red, white, yellow, orange, and black, which, though less appreciated, have their own unique beauty.

## 半透明ながら深い緑の琅玕

日本では縄文時代の遺跡からヒスイを加工した跡が見つかるほど、長い歴史があります。新潟県の糸魚川一帯が名産地として知られていました。

皇族と深いゆかりがある石でもあります。天孫降臨に際して授けられ、皇位とともに継承される三種の神器のうち、勾玉はヒスイで作られているといわれています。

良質のヒスイは、トロリとした色合いでありながら透明感があります。石を手に取り、ペンライトで横から光を当ててみると、良質であるほど光を通し、透明度が高いことがわかります。

色と透明度の両方を兼ね備え、半透明でありながら濃い緑色をしているのが「琅玕（ろうかん）」と呼ばれる最高級のヒスイです。「銀杏の実の色を濃くして、表面に油を流してトロリとさせた色」と表現され、「インペリアルジェード（皇帝のヒスイ）」との別名があります。

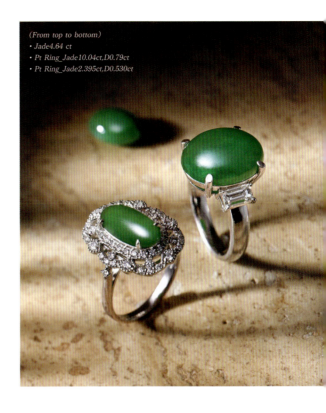

(From top to bottom)
- Jade 4.64 ct
- Pt Ring_Jade 10.04ct, D0.79ct
- Pt Ring_Jade 2.395ct, D0.530ct

## *Rokan*: Translucent and Deep Green Jadeite

Jade has a long history in Japan, with traces of jade craftsmanship found at Jomon-period archaeological sites. The Itoigata region in Niigata Prefecture was renowned as a major source of jade.

This stone is also deeply connected to the Japanese imperial family. According to Japanese mythology, the *magatama*, which is said to have been made from jade, is one of the Three Sacred Treasures handed down with each imperial succession. It was first bestowed upon the Sun Goddess's grandson when he descended to Earth to establish the imperial line.

High-quality jade has a rich, flowing color with a translucent quality. When held under a penlight from the side, the best jade reveals a high degree of translucency.

Jade with excellent color and translucency is considered the most prestigious, particularly the semi-translucent, deep green variety known as *rokan*. This top-tier jade has been described as having a "rich ginkgo nut color with an oily texture," and is also referred to as "Imperial Jade."

## Jade Color Grading Table

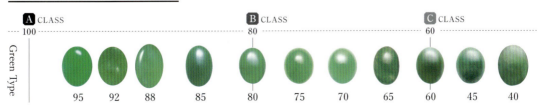

95点、92点のヒスイは半透明で見事な色合いの琅玕。透明度に欠け、色むらなどがあると評価が下がります。

Jadeite graded at 95 or 92 points is *rokan* of exceptional quality, characterized by its semi-translucent nature and remarkable color. Jadeite lacking translucency or with uneven coloration receives lower evaluations.

*(From top to bottom)*
- Pt Ring_Jade8.52ct,D0.631ct
- Pt Ring_Jade9.88ct,D0.708ct
- Pt Ring_Jade7.04ct,D0.52ct,Pallasite Peridot0.037ct/0.031ct

## 硬玉と軟玉の違いに注意

　中国の歴代王朝において、ヒスイが特別な存在であったことは広く知られています。なかでも清朝を全盛期へ導いた第6代皇帝乾隆帝は、ヒスイを産出するミャンマーの北部に国境を超えて侵攻し、朝貢国としました。

　現在でも中国ではヒスイへの思い入れが強く、家宝として受け継ぎ、多くの人が護符として携えています。日本では濃い緑色が人気であるのに対し、中国で高く評価されるのは明るめの緑色です。

　ヒスイに「硬玉（ジェダイト）」と「軟玉（ネフライト）」があることも覚えておきましょう。鉱物として別物であり、宝石のヒスイは輝石に属する硬玉です。価値に天地の差がある軟玉は、産出量が多く、彫刻などを施して工芸品に使われます。

## The Differences Between Jadeite and Nephrite

Jade was regarded as an extraordinary and cherished material throughout the dynasties of Chinese history. Notably, during the Qing Dynasty, Emperor Qianlong, the sixth ruler who led the dynasty to its height, launched military campaigns into northern Myanmar, a jade-producing region, and made it a tributary state.

Even today, jade holds deep cultural significance in China. It is often passed down as a family heirloom and carried by many as an amulet. While deep green jade is favored in Japan, lighter green colors are more highly valued in China.

It is also important to note the distinction between jadeite and nephrite, the two types of jade. These are mineralogically distinct, with gemstone-quality jade belonging to the pyroxene group as jadeite. Nephrite, in contrast, is less valuable, more abundant, and mainly used for carved ornaments and crafts.

# Jade

### パステル調の可憐な魅力

ヒスイには緑色のほか紫や赤、青などさまざまな色があり、緑色の次に人気が高いのがラベンダーヒスイです。パステル調の可愛らしい薄紫色は、鉄とチタン、マンガンなどの影響から生まれるといわれますが、完全には解明されていません。

ラベンダーヒスイには、アメリカ大陸で最も古い中米のオルメカ文明で珍重された歴史があり、現代のアメリカでは緑色より人気があります。

高く評価されるのは、ラベンダーの花のような美しい薄紫色。染色処理されることも多いため、注意が必要です。宝石質のものは主にミャンマーで産出されます。緑色より産出が格段に少なく、大変レアな存在です。

### Delicate Charm in Pastel Tones

In addition to green, jade comes in various colors such as purple, red, and blue. Among these, lavender jade is the second most popular after green jade. Its soft pastel lilac tone is believed to result from elements such as iron, titanium, and manganese, although the exact cause remains unknown.

Lavender jade has a long history, having been highly valued by the Olmec civilization, the oldest known culture in Mesoamerica. Today, it is even more popular than green jade in modern America.

The highly valued lavender jade exhibits a beautiful light purple color reminiscent of lavender flowers. However, since dyed lavender jade is common, caution is necessary. Gem-quality lavender jade is primarily mined in Myanmar. Its production is far rarer than that of green jade, making it an exceptionally rare find.

# Lavender Jade

ラベンダーヒスイ

*(From left to right)*
- Pt Pendant_Lavender Jade9.70ct,D0.46ct
- Pt Pendant_Lavender Jade5.626ct,D0.380ct
- Lavender Jade22.48ct

## Lavender Jade Color Grading Table

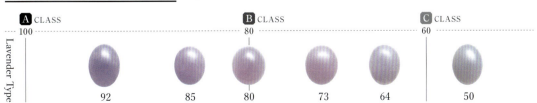

92点の石はラベンダーの花のような色合いが美しい逸品。紫が濃いほど評価が高く、白っぽくなるにつれ低くなります。

A 92-point stone is exceptional, showcasing a light purple tone reminiscent of lavender flowers. Deeper purples are valued higher, while paler or whitish tones are rated lower.

# Jade
## Production Trends and Value
ヒスイの産出動向とその価値

ヒスイの原石　Jade rough stone

　ヒスイは中国で産出されると誤解している人が少なくありませんが、実際に良質の石が産出されるのはミャンマーのみです。北部に位置するカチン州の山岳地帯にあるパーカン鉱山で、おもに採掘されています。

　ヒスイは大きな岩石の中に埋まっていて、良質の石かどうかを判断することは困難です。パーカン鉱山で採掘されると、一大集積地であるマンダレーまで岩石のまま運ばれ、取引されますが、岩のなかに素晴らしいヒスイが眠っているかどうかは岩を割ってみなければわかりません。

　琅玕クオリティのヒスイも、わずかながら産出が続いていますが、価格はとほうもなく高騰しています。中国の経済発展につれてヒスイの価格は全体に大きく上昇していき、良質の石を入手するのは困難になりました。かつては中国では好まれない色が濃すぎるヒスイを、日本の業者が買いつける機会もありましたが、近年ではそのようなチャンスも少なくなっています。

　さらに、アメリカやヨーロッパでもヒスイの人気が高まったことで、特級品である琅玕をはじめ、絶対量がますます足りなくなっています。

　ラベンダーヒスイについても、緑のヒスイと同じくミャンマーの鉱山で産出されます。産出量がもともと少ないうえ、人気が高まっているため、価格が上昇しています。

Many people mistakenly believe that jade is produced in China, but in reality, high-quality jade is only found in Myanmar. Most of it is mined in the mountainous regions of Kachin State in northern Myanmar, particularly at the Pakang mines.

Jade is embedded within large rocks, making it difficult to assess the quality of the stone at a glance. After being extracted from the Pakang mines, these rocks are transported to Mandalay, a major trading hub, where they are sold in their rough form. However, the true value of the jade is only revealed when the rocks are cut open to see whether exceptional stones lie inside.

While jade of *rokan* quality is still being mined, its production is extremely limited, and prices have skyrocketed. As China's economy has grown, jade prices have risen significantly overall, making it increasingly difficult to acquire high-quality stones. In the past, Japanese dealers were able to purchase jade that was considered too dark for the Chinese market, but such opportunities have become rare in recent years.

Additionally, the increasing popularity of jade in the United States and Europe has further worsened the shortage of top-tier jade, including *rokan*, leaving the global supply increasingly inadequate.

Lavender jade, like green jade, is also mined in Myanmar. However, with its naturally low production levels and increasing demand, its price has been steadily rising.

# 縄文人が愛したヒスイ

## Jade: Cherished by Jomon People

文・岡本敬人　Text by Takahito Okamoto

### 日本人のルーツに隠された平和のDNA

　縄文時代から、日本列島に住む人々は宝石を身に着けていたことがわかっています。縄文時代とひとくちに言ってもその期間はとても長く、諸説ありますが、今から約1万6500年前から約2400年前までの1万4000年以上の期間を指します。その時代に日本列島に暮らしていた人々が縄文人と呼ばれているのです。

　現在の新潟県糸魚川付近は、当時からヒスイの一大産地として知られており、人々は勾玉などを作り身に着けていました。

　日本の皇位継承に欠かせない三種の神器のひとつである八尺瓊勾玉も、ヒスイでできているといわれています。

　縄文人のDNAは同時代に大陸に暮らしていた人々から分岐しましたが、縄文の文化は、同時代の大陸での旧石器時代、新石器時代のものとは異なり、独自の進化をとげたことがわかってきているそうです。

　何が異なっていたのか……そのひとつは通年的に定住しながらも、縄文時代がとても「平和」だったということです。縄文時代の遺跡からは戦いの痕跡がほとんど見つかっておらず、争いが極めて少なかったことがわかります。

　縄文の人々はカラフルでデザイン性の高い服をまとい、性別や年齢を問わず、耳飾り、首輪、腕輪などを身に着け、中にはヒスイなどの宝石で作られた装飾品を身に着けている人もいました。縄文の人々は、宝石がもつエネルギーを自然と体感していたのではないかと私は考えています。

　私たちの祖先が、太古の昔から平和を愛し、宝石を活用していたことに想いをはせながら、日本から世界の皆さんに宝石の真価をお伝えしていきたいと思っています。

縄文時代のヒスイの勾玉
Jade *magatama* from the Jomon period
Photo by ColBase

### The Hidden DNA of Peace in the Japanese People

It is known that people in the Japanese archipelago have been wearing gemstones since the Jomon period. Though referred to as a single era, the Jomon period spans an exceptionally long time. While estimates vary, it is generally believed to have lasted for over 14,000 years, from approximately 16,500 years ago to about 2,400 years ago. The people who lived in the Japanese archipelago during this time are known as the Jomon people.

The region around present-day Itoigawa in Niigata Prefecture was already recognized as a major source of jade in those times. People crafted *magatama* (curved beads) and other ornaments from jade and wore them as accessories. Jade is also believed to be the material of the *Yasakani no Magatama*, one of the Three Sacred Treasures essential to Japan's imperial succession.

Genetic research suggests that the DNA of the Jomon people diverged from that of the people living on the continent at the same time. Their culture took a different path from the Paleolithic and Neolithic cultures of mainland Asia. It shaped itself independently, developing unique characteristics over time.

What made them different? One noteworthy aspect of the Jomon period was its peacefulness, despite the fact that they were permanently settled in one place. Archaeological sites from this era show almost no traces of warfare, indicating that conflict was extremely rare.

The Jomon people wore colorful, intricately designed clothing and adorned themselves with earrings, necklaces, and bracelets, regardless of age or gender. Some even wore jewelry made from jade and other gemstones. I believe they instinctively sensed the energy of gemstones and embraced it.

Reflecting on how our ancestors cherished peace and valued gemstones since ancient times, I hope to share the true essence of gemstones from Japan with people around the world.

(Top)
- Pt／YG Ring_Pink Diamond0.065ct,
  Yellow Diamond0.07ct,D0.27ct／YD0.07ct

(Middle row left to right)
- Pt／YG Tie tack_Yellow Diamond0.98ct,D1.185ct
- Pt Ring_Diamond1.80ct,D1.79ct
- YG Fancy-Colored Diamond Pendant_ Fancy-Colored Diamond
  0.38ct／0.37ct／0.09ct／0.05ct／0.18ct／0.19ct／0.39ct／0.34ct／
  0.44ct／0.18ct／0.36ct／0.54ct
- YG Fancy-Colored Diamond Pendant_
  0.578ct／0.16ct／0.13ct／0.10ct／0.09ct

(Lower row from left to right)
- Fancy Light Green Diamond1.01ct,
  Fancy Vivid Yellow-Orange Diamond0.79ct,
  Fancy Greenish Blue Diamond0.38ct

# Diamond

ダイヤモンド

## 万物のなかで最も硬い石

　はるか30数億年前、活発な火山活動の影響を受けて地中深くで生成されたダイヤモンド。鉛筆の芯と同じく炭素でできていながら、眩いばかりの輝きを放ち、人の心を魅了してきました。

　古代インドでは護符として珍重されたと伝えられます。中世ヨーロッパでは装身具に用いられ貴族の身を飾り、富と権力の象徴でもありました。

　語源は、ギリシャ語で「征服されない」を意味する「アダマス」。硬度が10と、万物のなかで最も硬い物質であることに由来します。

## The Hardest Stone in Existence

Over 3 billion years ago, diamonds were formed deep within the Earth under the influence of intense volcanic activity. Despite being composed of carbon, the same element found in pencil leads, diamonds captivate with their dazzling brilliance and have fascinated humanity for centuries.

　In ancient India, diamonds were treasured as protective amulets. During medieval Europe, they adorned the nobility, serving as symbols of wealth and power.

　The word "diamond" derives from the Greek word *adamas*, meaning "unconquerable." This name reflects its unparalleled hardness, rated as 10 on the Mohs scale, making it the hardest substance on Earth.

# Diamond

ダイヤモンド

## カットの生み出す底知れぬ煌めき

　ダイヤモンドの美しさと価値を大きく進化させたのが、カット技術の発展です。ブリリアントカットにつながるカットの原形は17世紀に考案され、20世紀になって大きく開花。58面体で構成される精緻なカットの研磨方法が確立され、揺るぎない人気と地位を得ることとなりました。息をのむ煌めきが数知れぬ人々を魅了し続けています。

　ダイヤモンドは品質、価値を決定する基準が明確に定められています。それが良く知られる「Color（色）」「Clarity（透明性）」「Cut（カット）」「Carat（重さ）」の「4C」です。それぞれに細分化された基準があり、専門機関により鑑定され、価格が決まるシステムが構築されています。

## The Boundless Brilliance Created by the Cut

The evolution of diamond cutting techniques has significantly enhanced both the beauty and value of diamonds. The precursor to the modern brilliant cut was conceived in the 17th century and reached its pinnacle in the 20th century. This advancement led to the creation of a precise cutting method with 58 facets, securing its unwavering status and enduring popularity. Its breathtaking sparkle continues to captivate countless admirers around the world.

　Diamonds are evaluated and valued according to clearly defined criteria, known as the "Four Cs": Color, Clarity, Cut, and Carat weight. Each of these categories is further divided into detailed standards and assessed by specialized institutions, creating a systematic approach to determining a diamond's price and quality.

*(Clockwise from top left)*
- Pt Ring_Diamond1.023ct
- WG Pendant_Diamond1.59ct
- Pt Ring_Diamond1.012ct,D0.77ct
- Pt Ring_Diamond2.89ct
- Diamond5.02ct

### ピンクダイヤのレアな輝き

　ダイヤモンドは無色以外にも豊富なカラーバリエーションがあります。レッド、ブルー、ピンク、パープル、グリーン、オレンジ、イエロー、ブラウンの順に価値が高く、特にレッド、ブルーはほとんど市場に出回ることはありません。

　天然のカラーダイヤモンドは、稀少価値が高く、その人気は絶大。発見される確率は、無色の一般的なダイヤモンドの1万分の1といわれています。なかでもピンクはその可憐な美しさと稀少性から人気が高く、2017年、サザビーズのオークションで59.6ctの「ピンクスター」が当時のレートで約79億円で落札され、話題になりました。

　イエローダイヤは、カラーダイヤの中では比較的お手頃ですが、オレンジに近い濃い色のものは高くなります。カラーダイヤモンドは色の濃さ、鮮やかさがおもな評価ポイントで、イエローなら黄色みが強いほど高評価です。

### The Rare Brilliance of Pink Diamonds

Diamonds are not limited to being colorless; they come in a wide range of colors, including red, blue, pink, purple, green, orange, yellow, and brown. They are ranked in this order of value, with red and blue being the rarest and almost never appearing on the market.

　Natural colored diamonds are extraordinarily rare and immensely popular. It is said that the chance of discovering a colored diamond is one in 10,000 compared to a typical colorless diamond. Among them, pink diamonds are especially coveted for their delicate beauty and rarity. In 2017, the "Pink Star," a 59.6-carat pink diamond, was sold at a Sotheby's auction for approximately 7.9 billion yen (about $71 million USD at the exchange rate of the time), drawing significant attention.

　Yellow diamonds are relatively affordable among colored diamonds, but those with a deeper, more orange tone are valued more highly. For colored diamonds, the richness and vibrancy of the color are key factors in determining their value. In the case of yellow diamonds, the stronger and more vivid the yellow, the higher the appraisal.

(From top to bottom)
- YG Ring_Yellow Diamond0.45ct,Diamond0.26ct
- Pt Ring_Yellow Diamond1.011ct,D0.43ct
- Pt Ring_Pink Diamond1.00ct,D1.256ct
- Fancy Light Orange-Pink Diamond0.72ct
- Fancy Intense Yellowish Orange Diamond0.50ct

# Pink Diamond & Yellow Diamond

ピンクダイヤモンド ＆ イエローダイヤモンド

# Blue Diamond & Green Diamond & Brown Diamond

ブルーダイヤモンド ＆ グリーンダイヤモンド ＆ ブラウンダイヤモンド

## 最も高い評価を受けるブルー

　カラーダイヤモンドのなかでも、幻の赤についで最も高く評価されるのがブルー。年に数個採れるかというほど数が少なく、その稀少価値ゆえ天文学的な価格となります。有名なブルーダイヤモンドに「ホープダイヤモンド」があり、さまざまな歴史と逸話に彩られています。

　グリーンダイヤモンドの色みはエメラルドグリーンからオリーブグリーンまであり、色が濃いほど評価されます。放射線に当たるという発生条件が整うことは稀で、それだけ稀少価値があります。

　ブラウンダイヤモンドはおもに工業用に用いられてきました。近年になり、チョコレートダイヤモンドと名づけて売り出され、話題になっています。

## The Most Highly Valued Blue

Among colored diamonds, blue diamonds are the second most highly valued after the elusive red diamond. With only a handful discovered each year, their extreme rarity drives their prices to astronomical levels. One of the most famous blue diamonds is the "Hope Diamond," a gem shrouded in rich history and captivating legends.

Green diamonds exhibit colors ranging from emerald green to olive green, with deeper shades commanding higher value. The conditions required for their formation—exposure to natural radiation—are exceptionally rare, contributing to their scarcity and high desirability.

Brown diamonds, traditionally used for industrial purposes, have recently gained attention under the rebranding of "Chocolate Diamond," creating a new market.

(From left to right)
- WG Pendant_Brown Diamond2.76ct, D2.68ct
- Fancy Light Grayish Blue Diamond0.64ct
- Fancy Light Blue Diamond0.50ct
- WG／PG Ring_Fancy Green Diamond1.19ct,PD0.13ct,D4.09ct

# Diamond
## Production Trends and Value
ダイヤモンドの産出動向とその価値

　無色のダイヤモンドの産出地は、おもにボツワナ、ナミビア、南アフリカ、シエラレオーネ、アンゴラなどアフリカの国々。ほかには、ロシア、カナダで採掘されたダイヤモンドが増えています。

　稀少価値の高いのは、カラーダイヤモンド。ピンクダイヤモンドについては、一級品のほとんどはオーストラリアのアーガイル鉱山で産出されます。しかし、ここも閉山してしまいました。

　ダイヤモンドは、世界基準にもとづいて評価され、細かく等級分けされ価格が設定されるという色石との違いがあります。これは世界市場をほぼ独占していたデビアス社が、価格をコントロールしてきたことも影響しています。

　4Cの何を基準にダイヤを選ぶかは、それぞれの価値観次第ですが、決まった予算の中で、より大きく見栄えする石がほしい場合は、カットとカラットを重視して選ぶことをおすすめします。

　カラーは自分の目で見て美しいと思えれば問題ありません。鑑定書でカラーが1〜2ランク下がっても、カットが良ければ美しさはあまり変わりません。カラーのランクを下げれば価格は下がりますから、同じ予算でより大粒の石を選ぶことができます。傷と内包物は輝きを阻害しますが、肉眼で確認できないならば美しさが大きく損なわれることはないでしょう。

The primary sources of colorless diamonds are African countries such as Botswana, Namibia, South Africa, Sierra Leone, and Angola. Additionally, diamonds from Russia and Canada are becoming increasingly prominent.

Colored diamonds, however, are far rarer and more valuable. Most top-grade pink diamonds were historically mined at the Argyle Mine in Australia, which has now closed, further elevating their scarcity.

Unlike colored gemstones, diamonds are evaluated and graded according to global standards, with prices set based on detailed criteria. This system was strongly influenced by De Beers, a company that historically dominated the global diamond market and controlled pricing.

When selecting a diamond, the aspect of the Four Cs to prioritize depends on individual preferences. If you wish to maximize size and visual appeal within a specific budget, it is advisable to focus on cut and carat weight.

The color grade is less critical as long as the diamond looks beautiful to the naked eye. Even if the certification indicates a color grade one or two levels lower, a high-quality cut ensures that the diamond's beauty remains largely unaffected. Choosing a lower color grade can also allow you to allocate your budget toward a larger stone. While inclusions and blemishes can impact a diamond's brilliance, they generally do not significantly detract from its overall beauty if they are not visible to the naked eye.

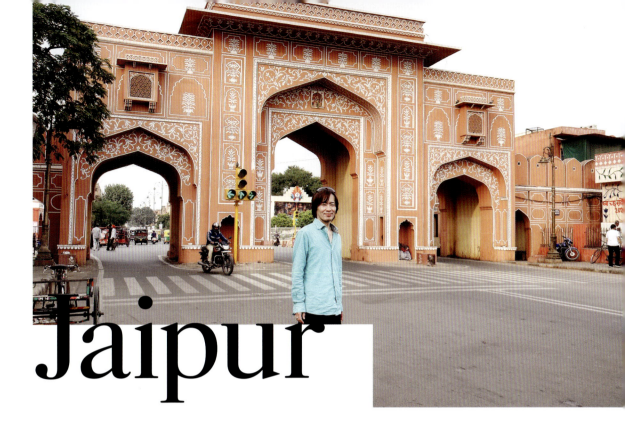

# Jaipur

## 世界の宝石が集まる
## 宝石の都・ジャイプール

Jaipur: The Gemstone Capital
Where the World's Jewels Gather

文・岡本敬人
Text by Takahito Okamoto

軒先で宝石のビーズを選別している様子

Sorting gemstone beads at the storefront

路地裏の店にも豪華なインドのジュエリーが飾られている

Even the back alley shops display luxurious Indian jewelry

### 街のいたるところで宝石が売買される

　インド北西部、ラジャスターン州の州都ジャイプールは、世界有数のカラーストーン集散地。ジャイプールにおける宝石産業の歴史は1700年代にまで遡ります。街を築いたアンベール王のジャイ・シンク2世によって腕のいい宝石職人、一流のジュエラーが呼び寄せられ、ジャイプールは今日まで続く宝石の街として発展を遂げていったの

### A City Where Gemstones Are Traded Everywhere

Jaipur, the capital of Rajasthan in northwestern India, is one of the world's major hubs for colored gemstones. The city's gemstone industry dates back to the 1700s when Maharaja Jai Singh II, the ruler of Amber, invited highly skilled gem artisans and renowned jewelers to settle there. Since then, Jaipur has flourished as a gemstone city, maintaining its status to this day.

　The city's main streets are lined with numerous jewelry shops. The largest gemstone store in

街中を歩いている象
An elephant walking down the street

研磨は分業制で行われている
Gemstone polishing is carried out through a division of labor

宝石をアルミホイルで包んで、チョークの粉の中に入れて加熱する
Wrapping gemstones in aluminum foil and heating them in chalk powder

です。

　ジャイプールのメインストリートには宝石店が数多く立ち並んでいます。街にある一番大きな宝石専門店はまるでデパートのような規模。さらにメインストリートのみならず、裏路地にもたくさんの宝石店や、宝石関係のお店が立ち並んでおり、宝石の街の奥深さが感じられます。

### 一大集積地のメリット

　ジャイプールには世界各国から様々な宝石の原石が集まり、腕の良い職人たちが研磨しています。工場の規模は大小様々です。今回案内してもらったのは、街の中心地にあるサンディープ・ラワット氏の一族が運営する宝石研磨工場。

　この工場では、研磨は基本的に工程ごとに分業で行われており、大まかな形を決める人、スティックに石をつける人、ラフなカットをする人など、ひとつのルースが仕上がるまで、平均15名程の

Jaipur is as vast as a department store. Beyond the main roads, even the back alleys are filled with jewelry stores and businesses related to the gemstone trade, highlighting the depth of Jaipur's gem industry.

### The Advantages of a Major Gemstone Hub

Jaipur attracts raw gemstones from all over the world, which are then cut and polished by skilled artisans. The city hosts a wide range of gem-cutting workshops, varying in size. On this visit, we were guided through a gemstone polishing workshop run by the family of Mr. Sandeep Rawat,

タンザニアから届いたタンザナイトの原石。この工場で加熱研磨される
Tanzanite rough stones from Tanzania. They are heated, cut, and polished in this workshop

職人が携わっています。ただし、大きく高価な石の場合は、腕のいい職人が1人で担当することもあるそうです。

ジャイプールには、ジュエリー工場が集まっている宝石工場地帯もあります。このエリアには30程の大小様々な宝石工場が集まっており、大きな工場では3000人程の職人が働いているそうです。

一大集積地であるジャイプールでは、高額な宝石から低価格のロットで使うものまで、すべての宝石を余すところなく加工して販売することができます。もし、クオリティーの高いものだけを扱っていたら、大きなロスが出るため、値段は当然高額になります。しかし、すべての宝石を有効活用できるジャイプールで研磨・加工するからこそ、クオリティーの高い宝石の値段も高くなりすぎずに取引が可能になっているのです。

原石をチェックする岡本氏
Mr. Okamoto inspecting rough gemstones

located in the heart of the city.

At this facility, the cutting and polishing process is divided into specialized tasks. Different artisans are responsible for shaping the rough stone, attaching it to a stick, and making the initial cuts. On average, around 15 artisans contribute to finishing a single loose gemstone. However, for larger and more valuable stones, a single highly skilled craftsman may handle the entire process.

Jaipur is also home to an industrial zone dedicated to jewelry manufacturing, where around 30 gemstone workshops of various sizes are concentrated. Some of the larger facilities employ up to 3,000 artisans.

As a major gemstone hub, Jaipur processes and sells everything from high-value gems to lower-priced stones used in bulk production. If only high-quality stones were selected for processing, a significant portion of raw materials would go to waste, driving up prices. However, Jaipur's ability to utilize all available gemstones ensures that even high-quality stones remain competitively priced in the market.

ジャイプールにて買い付けする岡本氏
Mr. Okamoto purchasing gemstones in Jaipur

宝石の色を分けるのは熟練の職人の眼
Sorting gemstones by color requires the keen eye of a skilled artisan

# Jaipur
世界の宝石が集まる
**宝石の都・ジャイプール**

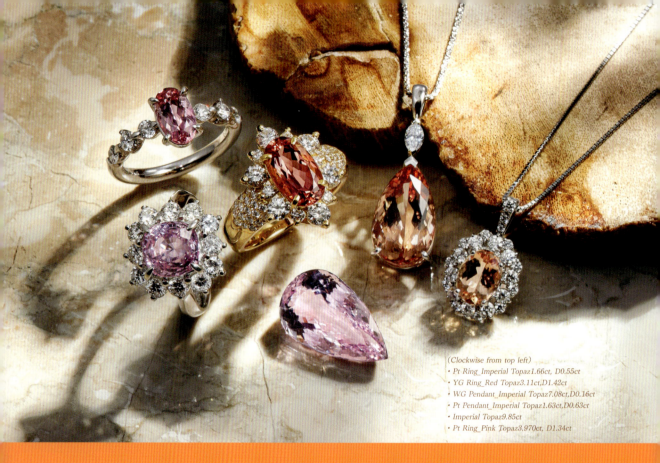

(Clockwise from top left)
- Pt Ring_Imperial Topaz1.66ct, D0.55ct
- YG Ring_Red Topaz3.11ct,D1.42ct
- WG Pendant_Imperial Topaz7.08ct,D0.16ct
- Pt Pendant_Imperial Topaz1.63ct,D0.63ct
- Imperial Topaz9.85ct
- Pt Ring_Pink Topaz3,970ct, D1.34ct

# Topaz

トパーズ

### 「火の石」「黄玉」と呼ばれる色石

　古代エジプトの時代から人々に愛されてきたトパーズ。古代ローマでは男性が好んで指輪にしたことが知られています。黄色の色合いから太陽神の象徴とされ、護符に用いられました。

　インドにおいても、その色合いから「火の石」と呼ばれ、サンスクリット語で火をあらわす「タパス」がトパーズの語源になったともいわれます。

　和名も「黄玉」。こうして見ると、トパーズは黄色と考えられてきたことがわかりますが、実際には赤からピンク、青など豊富な色みがあります。

### Gemstones Known as "Firestone" and "Yellow Gem"

Topaz has been cherished since the time of ancient Egypt. In ancient Rome, it was a popular choice for men's rings. Its golden color made it a symbol of the sun god and a material often used for amulets.

In India, topaz was referred to as the "firestone" due to its fiery color. It is believed that the name "topaz" may have originated from the Sanskrit word *tapas*, which means "heat" or "fire."

In Japanese, topaz is known as *kōgyoku*, or "yellow gem." This historical association with yellow demonstrates how topaz was traditionally perceived. However, in reality, it comes in a wide variety of colors, including red, pink, and blue.

# Imperial Topaz

インペリアルトパーズ

### トパーズの頂点に君臨

　トパーズのなかでも特に高い評価を受けるものは、インペリアルトパーズ、すなわち「皇帝のトパーズ」と呼ばれます。

　幅広い色合いがあるトパーズは、色による価値の違いが大きく、最高評価を受けるのは赤です。濃い赤色をしたインペリアルトパーズは、通称レッドトパーズと呼ばれ、非常に稀少で、価格もきわめて高くなっています。

　赤に次いで高く評価されるのが、極上のシェリー酒のようなややオレンジ色を帯びたシェリーカラー。その次に位置づけられるのが、ややオレンジがかった優しいピンク系と深みのあるイエロー系です。

　シェリーカラーのみならずピンクやイエローのインペリアルトパーズも世界的に人気が上昇し、それにつれて価格が上がっています。

*(From top to bottom)*
- *Pt Pendant_Imperial Topaz3.66ct,D0.36ct*
- *Pt Pendant_Imperial Topaz0.84ct,D0.18ct*
- *Imperial Topaz11.70ct*
- *Pt Ring_Red Topaz4.16ct,D0.42ct*
- *Pt Ring_Imperial Topaz1.72ct,D0.56ct*
- *Pt Ring_Imperial Topaz2.53ct,D0.27ct*

### Reigning at the Pinnacle of Topaz

Among topaz varieties, the most highly prized is Imperial Topaz, also known as the "Emperor's Topaz."

　Topaz comes in a wide range of colors, and its value varies significantly depending on its color. The most highly valued is red. Deep red Imperial Topaz, often referred to as "Red Topaz," is extremely rare and commands exceptionally high prices.

　The second most highly valued color is sherry, a rich tone reminiscent of fine sherry wine with a hint of orange. This is followed by soft pink tones with a slight orange tint and deep yellow shades, both of which are also highly regarded.

　In addition to sherry-colored topaz, pink and yellow Imperial Topaz have also been gaining global popularity, contributing to their increasing market value.

## Color variations

Red Type

Sherry Type

Yellow Type

レッドはルビーに似た鮮やかな赤であるほど評価が高くなります。
シェリーカラー、ピンク、イエローは色の濃度が濃いほど高評価。

The closer the red is to the vivid color of a ruby, the higher its value. For sherry, pink, and yellow colors, deeper saturation is regarded more highly.

# Pink Topaz & Bicolor Topaz

ピンクトパーズ & バイカラートパーズ

### 可憐なイメージのピンクトパーズ

ピンクトパーズは、やわらかな色合いと美しい輝きが女性に人気です。茶色がかった色が入らず、濃度が高く可憐なピンクが高く評価されます。

同じピンクの色石でも、サファイアなどと比べればピンクトパーズは大ぶりな石も手に入れやすいといえるでしょう。

2色の色が組み合わさっているのがバイカラートパーズです。自然が生み出す神秘だけに、産出される機会は非常に限られます。

ブラジル産のインペリアルトパーズの中に、ごく稀に見つかるのが、濃いシェリーレッドとイエローが混ざり合うバイカラートパーズ。なんともいえないグラデーションが美しく見る人を魅了しますが、非常にレアなコレクターズアイテムとなっています。

### The Sweet Charm of Pink Topaz

Pink topaz, with its soft tones and stunning brilliance, is particularly popular among women. The most highly valued stones are those with a vivid and delicate pink, free from brownish tones and possessing strong color saturation.

Compared to other pink gemstones, such as pink sapphire, pink topaz is often more affordable even in larger sizes, making it an attractive option for those seeking substantial gems.

A unique variation of topaz is bicolor topaz, which combines two distinct colors. As a natural marvel, its occurrence is extremely rare.

Among Brazilian Imperial Topaz, an exceptionally rare type of bicolor topaz is sometimes found, featuring a mesmerizing blend of deep sherry red and yellow. This exquisite gradient captivates viewers and has become a highly sought-after collector's item due to its rarity.

(Clockwise from top left)
- Pt Ring_Pink Topaz12.16ct,D1.45ct
- Bicolor Imperial Topaz7.97ct
- Bicolor Imperial Topaz5.98ct

## Color variations

Pink Topaz

可憐な印象のピンクが高評価。色の濃度が濃いほど価値が上がり、茶色がかった色みや薄いピンクではやや低くなります。

Sweet shades of pink are highly valued. The deeper the color saturation, the higher the value, while brownish or pale pink tones are considered less desirable.

# Topaz
## Production Trends and Value
トパーズの産出動向とその価値

トパーズは全体として見ると、比較的大粒の石が流通しています。ただし、最も高い評価を受ける赤いインペリアルトパーズは、小さいものでも稀にしか産出されず、大粒のものにはほとんどお目にかかれません。産出地はブラジルのミナス・ジェライス州の一部の地区です。

インペリアルトパーズは、ブラジルが産出の中心です。濃い色のシェリーカラーは産出量が少なくなっています。

ほかに、ロシア、タンザニア、マダガスカルなどでもトパーズは産出されています。産出が続いてはいるものの、人気の広がりによって価格も上がっています。

トパーズの価値を考える際は、色石全般と同じく3つの評価ポイントに注目します。色と内包物、輝きの3点です。

色は濃くなればなるほど評価が上がりますが、

Map of Topaz-Producing Countries
※おもな産出国や地域を記載しています
※Main producing countries and regions

最高の色を通り過ぎて黒味を帯びてくるとマイナスの評価を受けます。内包物は少なければ少ないほど評価は高くなりますが、目立つ場所になければさほど気にしなくてもいいでしょう。輝きについてはどれだけ美しいかをチェックします。

Topaz is generally available in relatively large sizes. However, red Imperial Topaz, the most highly valued variety, is exceptionally rare, even in smaller sizes, and large stones are almost unheard of. This rare variety is primarily found in specific areas of the Minas Gerais state in Brazil.

Brazil remains the central producer of Imperial Topaz, but the production of deep sherry-colored stones has decreased significantly.

Topaz is also mined in other countries, including Russia, Tanzania, and Madagascar. Although mining continues, the growing popularity of topaz has driven prices higher.

When evaluating the value of topaz, the same three key factors used for colored gemstones are considered: color, inclusions, and brilliance.

The richer the color, the higher the value, but if the color becomes overly dark or takes on a blackish tone, it can negatively impact the stone's rating. Inclusions, while best minimized, are not a major concern unless they are in prominent locations. As for brilliance, the overall beauty of the gem's sparkle is an essential consideration.

*(From left to right)*
- WG Pendant_Tanzanite6.94ct,D0.07ct
- Pt Pendant_Cab Tanzanite16.96ct,D0.92ct
- Pt Pendant_Tanzanite13.03ct,D1.86ct
- Pt Ring_Tanzanite7.04ct,D1.34ct
- Tanzanite21.13ct

# Tanzanite

タンザナイト

### キリマンジャロの暮れなずむ空の色

　タンザナイトは1970年、アフリカの名峰キリマンジャロをあおぐタンザニアのメレラニ鉱山で発見されました。
　その魅力をいち早く捉え、ロマンあふれる命名をしたのがアメリカのティファニー社でした。夕暮れ時に青紫色から群青色へ変わりゆく空を彷彿させるとして「タンザニアの夜」を意味するタンザナイトと名づけたのです。大々的なプロモーションが功を奏し、1980年代に全米で大ヒット。2021年には、日本の12月の誕生石にも追加され、その人気はさらに高まっています。

### The Colors of the Setting Sky over Kilimanjaro

Tanzanite was discovered in 1970 at the Merelani mines in Tanzania, near the base of Africa's iconic Mount Kilimanjaro.
　The gemstone's allure was quickly recognized by Tiffany & Co., the American jewelry house that gave it its romantically evocative name. They named it "Tanzanite," meaning "the night of Tanzania," inspired by the twilight sky over Tanzania, which shifts from blue-violet to deep blue. Their extensive promotional efforts proved successful, leading to a massive hit across the United States in the 1980s. In 2021, Tanzanite was officially added as a December birthstone in Japan, further elevating its status and appeal.

Tanzanite

(From top to bottom)
- Pt Ring_Tanzanite15.71ct,D1.00ct
- Pt Ring_Cab Tanzanite17.71ct,D0.88ct
- Pt Pendant_Tanzanite25.89ct,D1.17ct
- Pt Pendant_Cab Tanzanite10.82ct,D1.00ct
- WG Pendant_Fancy-Colored Tanzanite4.95ct,D0.27ct

# Tanzanite

タンザナイト

## 光の加減、見る角度で変わる表情

　タンザナイトの大きな特徴のひとつが多色性です。これは見る角度、当たる光の種類や加減により、青みが変化する性質のこと。自然光では透明感のある深い青色でありながら、白熱灯のもとでは紫色が優位になるといった異なる表情、変化が楽しめます。石によっては、群青色から濃い紫色、赤色が射し込む場合もあります。

　鉱物学上はゾイサイトという鉱物に属す石で、一般的なタンザナイトは約650℃で加熱処理を施すことで青紫色に変色します。近年になり、非加熱でも美しい石が発見され、ノーヒートタンザナイトと呼ばれています。非加熱で色が淡いものはファンシーカラータンザナイトといいます。

　また、最近は、150℃程度の低温で長時間、ゆっくりと加熱し、カボションカットにしたタンザナイトも人気があります。

## A Gemstone That Changes Its Appearance with Light and Viewing Angle

One of Tanzanite's key characteristics is its pleochroism, which causes its blue tones to shift depending on the viewing angle or the type and intensity of light. Under natural light, it displays a deep, transparent blue, while under incandescent light (white heat lamp), violet tones become dominant. Some stones may even show shades of ultramarine, deep violet, or hints of red.

　Tanzanite belongs to the mineral family of zoisite. Most Tanzanite is heat-treated at around 650°C to achieve its iconic blue-violet color. Recently, naturally beautiful stones that do not require heat treatment have been discovered and are called "no-heat Tanzanite." Stones with lighter, untreated colors are referred to as "fancy-colored Tanzanite."

　In addition, Tanzanite gently heated at lower temperatures—around 150 °C—over a long period and cut into cabochons has also become increasingly popular.

## Color variations

### No-Heat

### Heated

### Fancy-Colored Type

### Cabochon Cut

珍しいバイカラータンザナイト
Rare bicolor Tanzanite

色が濃いほど評価が高くなります。内包物が少ないほど透明感が増し、美しさが際立ちます。

The deeper the color, the higher the value. Fewer inclusions increase transparency, enhancing the gem's overall beauty.

# Tanzanite
## Production Trends and Value
タンザナイトの産出動向とその価値

タンザナイトが産出されるのは、タンザニア北部にあるメレラニ鉱山のみ。現在はまだある程度産出しており、世界的に流通していますが、産出がメレラニ鉱山のみのため、数十年後には産出しなくなる可能性が極めて高いとされています。もともと絶対量が限られていますから、人気が高まれば高まるほど市場に流通する量は減り、価格は高騰すると考えられます。

はじめに発見された当初よりも地中深いところまで採掘を進めるようになり、見つかったのがノーヒートタンザナイトです。人工的に加熱処理を施さなくとも、マグマにより自然に加熱され、美しい青色になった石です。稀少価値が非常に高いため、一般的なタンザナイトより価格が高く、今後ますます高騰することが見込まれます。

非加熱で淡い色合いのファンシーカラータンザナイトについては、産出量は多くありません。

Map of Tanzanite-Producing Country

輝きとテリが強く、透明感あふれる色合いの石が高く評価されます。

一般的なタンザナイトについては、以前に比べて多色性が重視されるようになったという変化があります。かつてはブルーサファイアに似た青色が高く評価されましたが、近年はさまざまな色み、色の変化のある石が評価されています。

Tanzanite is mined exclusively at the Merelani mines in northern Tanzania. While production continues and the gemstone is distributed globally, its reliance on a single mining site means that production is highly likely to cease within a few decades. With its limited supply, growing popularity is expected to reduce availability on the market and drive prices higher.

As mining has progressed to deeper layers, "no-heat Tanzanite" has been discovered. These stones naturally acquired their vivid blue color through exposure to magma without artificial heat treatment. Their extreme rarity makes them significantly more expensive than standard Tanzanite, with prices expected to rise further.

Fancy-colored Tanzanite, characterized by its pale, natural colors without heat treatment, is also produced in limited quantities. Stones with strong brilliance, vivid luster, and exceptional transparency are particularly valued.

In recent years, the criteria for evaluating Tanzanite have shifted. Previously, stones with a blue tone resembling blue sapphire were most highly valued. Today, Tanzanite with various colors and noticeable color shifts is gaining greater appreciation.

(From left to right)
- Inca Rose 7.20ct
- Pt Tie Tack_Inca Rose 6.10ct, D1.36ct
- Pt Pendant_Inca Rose 2.69ct, D0.86ct
- WG Pendant_Inca Rose 5.17ct, D0.196ct
- Pt Ring_Inca Rose 3.66ct, D1.15ct

# Inca Rose

インカローズ

## インカ文明とともに輝いた宝石

濃い蛍光ピンクが鮮烈なインパクトで胸に迫るインカローズ。独特のネオンカラーと煌めきは「ピンクのパライバトルマリン」とたたえられることもあります。ネーミングの由来は産出地。インカ帝国が栄えたアンデス山脈で13世紀には採掘が始まり、地元の人々に珍重されたことから「インカのバラの石」をあらわす名前がつきました。文明の衰退とともに採掘も途絶えてしまいました。

鉱物学では「ロードクロサイト」、ギリシャ語で「バラ色の石」をあらわします。

## A Gemstone That Shone Alongside the Inca Civilization

The striking fluorescent pink of Inca Rose leaves a vivid impression. Its distinctive neon color and brilliance have earned it the nickname "Pink Paraiba Tourmaline."

The name "Inca Rose" comes from its place of origin. Mining began in the Andes Mountains, the heart of the Inca Empire, as early as the 13th century. Treasured by local communities, the gemstone was named "The Rose of the Incas." However, mining came to a halt with the decline of the Inca Empire.

In mineralogical terms, the gemstone is called rhodochrosite, derived from the Greek word meaning "rose-colored stone."

Inca Rose

## 宝石質の石はきわめて稀少

インカローズは宝石のクオリティに達する石が非常に少ないという特徴があります。

和名は「菱マンガン鉱」。昔からマンガンを採る石として取り扱われ、そのなかに美しいピンク色を帯びたものが混ざっていました。

19世紀初頭にはルーマニアでも発見され、ヨーロッパで人気を呼びました。ただし、やはり良質の石は少なく、白い内包物を多く含む石がアクセサリーなどに用いられるに過ぎませんでした。

ですから20世紀になって透明度の高いピンクの石が「インカローズ」の名前で宝石市場に登場した時は、驚きをもって迎えられ大変な人気となったのです。きっかけは、アメリカ・コロラド州のスイートホーム鉱山で、良質の非常に美しいインカローズが採掘されたこと。透明度が高く鮮やかな蛍光を帯びたピンク色の宝石は、またたく間に世界的な人気となりました。この鉱山は残念ながら閉山し、良品はますます高騰しています。

## Gem-Quality Stones Are Extremely Rare

One of the defining features of Inca Rose is the extreme rarity of stones that reach gem quality.

Historically, rhodochrosite—its mineral name—was primarily mined for manganese, with occasional pink-colored stones found among the ore.

In the early 19th century, it was also discovered in Romania and later gained popularity in Europe. However, high-quality stones were extremely rare, and most of the material used for accessories contained significant white inclusions.

In the 20th century, the appearance of transparent, vibrant pink stones under the name "Inca Rose" created a sensation in the gem market. This breakthrough was driven by the discovery of exceptionally beautiful stones at the Sweet Home Mine in Colorado, USA. These gemstones, with their high transparency and vivid fluorescent pink color, quickly gained worldwide popularity. Unfortunately, the Sweet Home Mine has since closed, and as availability declines, the value of high-quality Inca Rose continues to rise.

### Color variations

蛍光ピンクの輝きがポイント。内包物はもともと多く、美しさを損なっていなければさほど気にする必要はありません。

The fluorescent pink brilliance is the key highlight. While inclusions are common, they are not a significant concern as long as they do not detract from the stone's overall beauty.

(From top to bottom)
- YG Pendant_Inca Rose3.05ct,D0.19ct
- WG Pendant_Inca Rose4.16ct,D0.34ct
- Pt Pendant_Inca Rose4.49ct,D0.28ct
- Inca Rose7.27ct

# Inca Rose
## Production Trends and Value

インカローズの産出動向とその価値

(From left to right)
- YG Pendant_Inca Rose3.68ct,YD0.27ct
- Pt Pendant_Inca Rose6.06ct,D0.72ct
- Pt Tie Tack_Inca Rose3.35ct,YD0.32ct,D0.17ct

アメリカ・コロラド州のスイートホーム鉱山で良品が採掘され、ピンクの美しい輝きを世界に知らしめたインカローズ。日本でも大変な人気となりましたが、この鉱山はすでに閉山。かつて採掘された原石が研磨され、市場に出回っている状況にあります。当然ながら、稀少価値は高まる一方で、価格は高騰を続けています。

インカローズは透明度が高く、鮮やかなピンク色のものが高く評価されます。インカの名前のルーツもある南米のペルー、アルゼンチンでも産出はあるものの、宝石のクオリティに達する質の高い石はごく一部に限られています。

また、中国でも産出はありますが、色みの薄いものが多いという特徴があります。

### Map of Inca Rose-Producing Countries

※おもな産出国や地域を記載しています
※Main producing countries and regions

Inca Rose gained worldwide recognition for its beautiful pink brilliance after high-quality stones were mined at the Sweet Home Mine in Colorado, USA. It also became very popular in Japan. However, the mine has since closed, and the market now relies on cut and polished stones from previously mined rough material. As a result, its rarity continues to grow, and prices keep rising.

The most highly valued Inca Rose has high transparency and vivid pink colors. While the gemstone is also mined in South American countries like Peru and Argentina—connected to its Inca-inspired name—only a small portion of the stones from these areas reach gem quality.

In China, Inca Rose is also mined, but the stones are often lighter in color, making them less valued in the market.

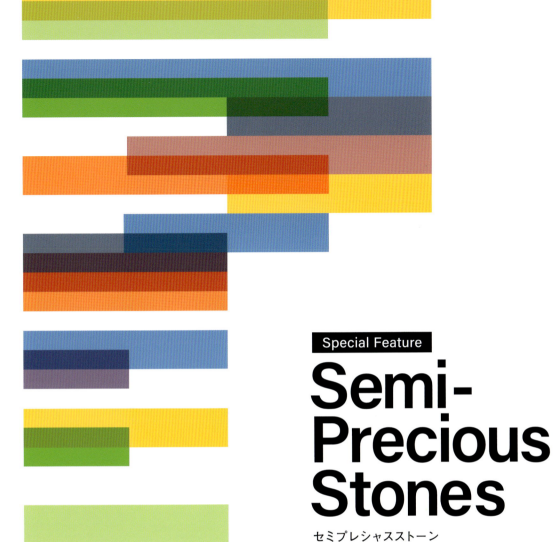

Special Feature

# Semi-Precious Stones

セミプレシャスストーン

　日本語では「半貴石」といわれるセミプレシャスストーン。ルビー、サファイアなどがプレシャスストーン、すなわち「貴石」であるのに対して、ワンランク下であるようなネーミングですが、それは必ずしも正しくありません。今最も高価といってもいいパライバトルマリンや稀少性と価値の高さで有名なデマントイドガーネットも半貴石です。この分類は石の硬度や採掘されてからの歴史が関係しているのです。

　いずれも地球が悠久の歴史のなかで育んだ特別な贈り物。その豊かな煌めきで世界的に人気のセミプレシャスストーンを紹介しましょう。

The term "semi-precious stones" might give the impression that they are of lower rank than precious stones like rubies and sapphires. However, this is not quite accurate. Paraiba tourmaline, considered one of the most valuable gemstones today, and demantoid garnet, celebrated for its rarity and high value, are also classified as semi-precious stones. This classification is influenced by factors such as hardness and the historical context of their discovery.

　These stones are extraordinary gifts from the Earth, formed over countless millennia. Let us introduce some globally popular semi-precious stones, admired for their stunning brilliance and rich beauty.

133

Semi-Precious Stone

# Aquamarine

アクアマリン

(From top left to right)
- PG Ring_Aquamarine2.04ct,D0.23ct
- Aquamarine2.43ct

(From the middle to the bottom)
- Pt Ring_Aquamarine0.79ct,D0.27ct
- Pt Ring_Aquamarine3.51ct,D0.84ct
- Pt Pendant_Aquamarine4.53ct,D0.34ct

## 海の神話に彩られた涼感あふれるマリンブルー

　浜辺に流れ着いた海の精の宝物が宝石になったとの神話が伝わるアクアマリン。「海の水」という意味のネーミングは、およそ2000年前、古代ローマ人によるといわれます。

　涼やかな透明感ある青に海を思うのは、古今東西変わらない人間の心情なのでしょう。マリンブルーの煌めきが心をとらえて離しません。

## A Refreshing Marine Blue Imbued with the Myths of the Sea

According to myth, aquamarine was a treasure of sea spirits washed ashore. Its name, meaning "water of the sea," was coined by the ancient Romans around 2,000 years ago.

　The cool, transparent blue of aquamarine evokes the ocean, a timeless sentiment shared across cultures. Its shimmering marine blue continues to captivate hearts.

## 「サンタマリア」と呼ばれる濃い青の最上のアクアマリン

アクアマリンはヨーロッパで、はるか昔から貴族に愛されました。昼間の涼し気な表情と打って変わり、夜にはキラキラと強く輝く特性があり、貴婦人が好んで夜会で身に着けたといわれます。中世には船乗りが航海のお守りとして携えました。

鉱物学的にはエメラルドと同じベリルに属し、入り込んだ微量の鉄分により青い色が生まれます。鉄分の入り方、量の微妙な違いで色合いに幅があり、濃いほうが高く評価されます。

色の濃い最上のアクアマリンは「サンタマリア」の称号で呼ばれます。代表的産出地ブラジルでも特に良品が採れるミナス・ジェライス州の鉱山名にちなんでつけられました。その後、モザンビーク、マダガスカルでも質の高いものが見つかり、産地の別なく最上の品に用いられています。

ブラジル、マダガスカルでは順調に産出が続いていますが、大粒のものは価格が上がっています。

## Santa Maria: The Finest Aquamarine in Deep Blue

Aquamarine has been cherished by European nobility for centuries. It is said that noblewomen favored aquamarine for evening events, as its cool, gentle appearance during the day transformed into a dazzling brilliance at night. In the Middle Ages, sailors carried it as a talisman for safe voyages.

Mineralogically, aquamarine belongs to the beryl family, like emerald. Its blue color is caused by trace amounts of iron, with subtle differences in the concentration of iron creating variations in color. Deeper blue tones are especially prized and valued more highly.

The finest aquamarine, with its rich, deep blue color, is known as Santa Maria. This name originates from a mine in Minas Gerais, Brazil, famous for producing exceptional stones. Later, high-quality aquamarine was also discovered in Mozambique and Madagascar, and Santa Maria now refers to the finest stones regardless of their origin.

Aquamarine continues to be mined steadily in Brazil and Madagascar, but the price of larger stones has been increasing in recent years.

(Clockwise from left)
- Pt Ring_Aquamarine1.65ct, D0.20ct
- Pt Pendant_Aquamarine1.50ct, D0.28ct
- Aquamarine15.40ct

## Color variations

Santa Maria

Aquamarine

サンタマリアの青の濃度の高さは一目瞭然。普通のアクアマリンも、色が濃いほど高く評価されます。

The deep blue intensity of Santa Maria aquamarine is unmistakable. Even with standard aquamarine, deeper colors are consistently more highly valued.

## Map of Aquamarine-Producing Countries

※おもな産出国や地域を記載しています
※Main producing countries and regions

Semi-Precious Stone

# Peridot

ペリドット

(Clockwise from top left)
- YG Tie Tack_ Peridot14.09ct
- YG Pendant_Peridot8.352ct,Pallasite Peridot0.498ct／0.051ct
- YG Pendant_Peridot2.320ct,D0.03ct
- YG Pendant_Cab Peridot2.50ct,D0.01ct

## クレオパトラに愛された
## オリーブのような独特の色とテリ

　オリーブの実に似て、オイルを塗ったような独特のテリのある黄緑色の石ペリドット。鉱物名のオリビン、和名の「かんらん石」、そのいずれもオリーブをさしています。

　ペリドットは古代のエジプト王朝で珍重され、王冠に配されたことが知られています。古代エジプト最後の女王となったクレオパトラにも、こよなく愛されていました。

## Loved by Cleopatra: A Unique Olive Color and Radiant Luster

Resembling an olive with its unique yellow-green color and oily luster, peridot is a gemstone of distinctive charm. Its mineral name, olivine, comes from its olive-like appearance.

　Peridot was highly prized in ancient Egypt and was often used to decorate royal crowns. It is famously known as a favorite gem of Cleopatra, the last queen of ancient Egypt.

(From left to right)
- WG／YG Pendant_Peridot2.97ct,Blue Spinel0.64ct, Pink Sapphire0.88ct,D0.54ct
- Pt Pendant_Peridot4.520ct,Yellow Sapphire0.26ct, Green Garnet0.09ct,D0.04ct
- Peridot41.31ct

## 複屈折率の高さによりあらわれるモザイク模様の色の濃淡

独特のオイリーな黄緑色は、石の主成分である第一鉄の影響によります。ただし、第一鉄が美しい緑色になることは稀であり、ペリドットに限って不可思議なマジックが働いたといえるでしょう。独特なテリと鮮やかさは、微量に含まれるクロムにより生まれるといわれています。

大きな特徴に複屈折率の高さがあり、肉眼でも石の裏面が二重に見えます。光の反射と屈折によるモザイク模様の美しさもチェックポイントです。

ブラジル、パキスタン、アフガニスタン、ミャンマーなどで安定した産出が続いており、なかでもミャンマー産は美しい石が多く価格も手頃です。

## Mosaic Patterns of Light and Shade Created by High Birefringence

The distinct oily yellow-green color of peridot is attributed to ferrous iron, the stone's main component. However, it is rare for ferrous iron to produce such a beautiful green color, making it seem as though a mysterious magic works exclusively in peridot. Its unique luster and vivid color are also thought to result from trace amounts of chromium.

One of peridot's defining features is its high birefringence, which causes the back facets of the stone to appear doubled to the naked eye. The mosaic pattern created by light reflection and refraction further enhance its beauty and is a key point to observe.

Peridot is steadily mined in Brazil, Pakistan, Afghanistan, and Myanmar. Myanmar, in particular, is known for producing exceptionally beautiful stones that are also relatively affordable.

## Color variations

黄緑から緑色まで幅広い色相。内包物が少なく、褐色みがない緑色で色が濃く、テリが強いほど高評価。透明度とカットも重要。

A wide range of colors from yellow-green to green. Stones with fewer inclusions, deeper green tones free of brownish shades, and a stronger luster are highly valued. Transparency and the quality of the cut are also key factors.

## Map of Peridot-Producing Countries

※おもな産出国や地域を記載しています
※Main producing countries and regions

キラキラとまばゆく輝く
虹色の光のイリュージョン

　見る角度により異なる色合いを帯びる多色性と、高い複屈折率による華やかな煌めきが魅力。ダイヤモンドをしのぐ光の分散で、ファセット（面）ごとに異なる色合いに輝き、ファイアと呼ばれる虹色の光のイリュージョンが楽しめます。石の色相は淡い黄色、緑、褐色など幅広く、石の裏面まで見通せる透明度の高さも特徴。人気が高まり、2021年に日本の7月の誕生石に制定されました。

Semi-Precious Stone

# Sphene
スフェーン

## A Dazzling Display of Rainbow-Colored Light

The allure of this gemstone lies in its pleochroism, which creates shifting colors depending on the viewing angle, and its high birefringence, resulting in dazzling brilliance. With light dispersion surpassing even that of diamonds, each facet shines in a different color, producing a rainbow-like illusion of light known as "fire."

　The gemstone is available in a wide range of colors, including pale yellow, green, and brown, and is notable for its exceptional transparency, allowing the back facets to be clearly visible. Its growing popularity led to its designation in 2021 as one of the birthstones for July in Japan.

*(From top to bottom)*
- WG Ring_Sphene11.96ct,D0.65ct
- Pt Ring_Sphene10.52ct,D1.006ct
- YG Pendant_Sphene16.40ct,D0.43ct
- Sphene15.50ct

## イエロー系もグリーン系も
## 煌めきの強さがポイント

スフェーンの鉱物名はチタナイト。推察される通り、銀灰色の金属チタンが含有されているためです。スフェーンという宝石名は、ギリシャ語でくさびを意味する「スフェノス」に由来し、くさび石という別名もあります。こちらは石の結晶がくさび状であることにちなんでいます。

スフェーンに幅広い色みがあるのは、チタンのほか鉄、マンガン、クロムなどが微妙な割合で入り込んでいるためです。全般的に鉄分が強く影響して、褐色化する傾向が見られます。

産出地による色みの違いもあります。主な産出地はブラジルとマダガスカルで、ブラジル産は褐色イエロー系の石が多く、マダガスカル産ではグリーン系の石が多く見られます。

スフェーンを選ぶ際は、輝きとインパクトの強さを大きなポイントとしてチェックし、色みについては好みで決めるといいでしょう。

## Whether Yellow or Green, Brilliance is Key

The mineral name of sphene is titanite, named for its content of the silvery-gray metal titanium. The gemstone name "sphene" originates from the Greek word *sphenos*, meaning "wedge," which also gives it the alternative name "wedge stone" due to its wedge-shaped crystal formations.

Sphene's broad spectrum of colors results from varying amounts of elements such as titanium, iron, manganese, and chromium. A higher iron content generally gives the stone a brownish tone.

Color variations also depend on the place of origin. The primary sources of sphene are Brazil and Madagascar. Brazilian sphene often features brownish-yellow tones, while sphene from Madagascar is more likely to exhibit green colors.

When choosing sphene, brilliance and its impact are key factors to consider, while the choice of color can be left to personal preference.

### Color variations

Green Type

Yellow Type

輝きの強さが評価のポイントとなる宝石。光や角度により黄色、オレンジ、赤などの色が美しく楽しめるものを選びましょう。

Brilliance is the key factor in evaluating this gemstone. Opt for one that displays vibrant tones of yellow, orange, or red, depending on the light and viewing angle.

### Map of Sphene-Producing Countries

※おもな産出国や地域を記載しています
※Main producing countries and regions

(From left to right)
- YG Pendant_Sphene4.88ct,D0.24ct
- YG Pendant_Sphene9.26ct,PD0.19ct,D0.83ct
- YG Pendant_Sphene4.532ct,D0.253ct

(From left to right)
- Royal Blue Moonstone20.08ct
- Pt Ring_Royal Blue Moonstone5.59ct,D1.64ct
- Pt Pendant_Royal Blue Moonstone3.45ct,D0.06ct
- Pt Pendant_Royal Blue Moonstone3.78ct,D0.33ct

Semi-Precious Stone

# Royal Blue Moonstone

ロイヤルブルームーンストーン

## 夜空に浮かぶ月の光を掌中で愛でられる奇跡の石

　冴えた夜空に月の光が浮かんでいるようなロイヤルブルームーンストーン。美しい夜の光景がとじ込められた神秘の石は、古来、人々を魅了し、ロマンをかき立ててきました。

　古代ギリシャでは「月の神々の力が宿る石」、古代ローマでは「月の光が固まった石」と信奉され、インドでは「宇宙の光を凝縮した石」として語り継がれてきたのです。

## A Miraculous Gemstone: Moonlight from the Night Sky in Your Hands

The Royal Blue Moonstone resembles the light of the moon floating in a clear night sky. This mystical gemstone, capturing the beauty of a nocturnal scene, has fascinated people throughout history and stirred their sense of romance and wonder.

In ancient Greece, it was revered as "a stone imbued with the power of the moon gods." In ancient Rome, it was believed to be "solidified moonlight," while in India, it was described as "a stone that condenses the light of the cosmos."

## インドでのみ産出された最高評価のきわめてレアな存在

ムーンストーンというと主流は乳白色。その大きな特徴が、ミルキーな色や時に青などの線が浮かぶシーン効果です。これは独特の内部構造によるもので、カリウムを多く含む正長石とナトリウムを多く含む曹長石（そうちょうせき）が交互に薄い層状に重なり、そこに光が当たって幻想的な効果を生み出します。

石全体を濃い青が支配するロイヤルブルームーンストーンは、インドでのみ産出される石に与えられた最高級の称号です。そこに虹のような光が加わったものは、レインボーロイヤルブルームーンストーンと呼ばれ、さらに稀少性が高く、価格も非常に高くなっています。

インドの産出地は近年、立ち入りができない状況が続き、ミャンマーで小粒なロイヤルブルー系が少量見つかり、期待されています。スリランカ産、タンザニア産の石は青の濃度がやや薄く、単にブルームーンストーンと呼ばれます。

## A Rare Gem of the Highest Quality, Found Only in India

The most common type of moonstone is milky white, known for its schiller effect, where milky tones or blue lines appear. This effect is caused by its unique structure: thin, alternating layers of potassium-rich orthoclase and sodium-rich albite interact with light to create a mesmerizing glow.

Royal Blue Moonstone, characterized by its deep blue color, is the highest-grade designation given to stones mined exclusively in India. If a rainbow-like iridescence is present, it is called "Rainbow Royal Blue Moonstone," which is even rarer and more expensive.

Access to Indian mining sites has been restricted in recent years. Small royal blue stones have been found in Myanmar, offering some hope for future supply. Stones from Sri Lanka and Tanzania, with lighter blue colors, are referred to simply as Blue Moonstone.

## Color variations

ロイヤルブルームーンストーンは青の濃度と透明感が評価のポイント。鉱物学的に異なる石が流通しているので注意が必要。

Royal Blue Moonstone is evaluated based on the depth of its blue color and its translucent clarity. Attention should be paid, as mineralogically different stones are also in circulation.

## Map of Royal Blue Moonstone-Producing Country

インド
India

*(From left to right)*
- *Royal Blue Moonstone 46.51ct*
- *Royal Blue Moonstone 9.09ct*
- *WG Pendant_Royal Blue Moonstone 5.80ct, Sapphire 0.46ct, D 0.85ct*

Semi-Precious Stone

# Sphalerite
スファレライト

(Clockwise from top left)
- WG Pendant_Sphalerite13.21ct,D0.386ct
- Pt Pendant_Sphalerite17.28ct,D0.37ct
- Sphalerite3.09ct
- YG Pendant_Sphalerite7.40ct, Paraiba Tourmaline0.25ct,D0.17ct

## オレンジから緑まで幅広い色相
## やわらかいのでペンダントに

　スファレライトは激しいまでの圧倒的な煌めきで、見る人の目をくぎ付けにする宝石です。その理由は、ダイヤモンドにひけをとらない高い屈折率に加え、ダイヤモンドの4倍にも上る光の分散率を誇るところにあります。

　光を当てるとギラギラと輝き、ファセット（面）にファイアと呼ばれる虹色の光があらわれます。

　硬度が3.5～4と低く、もろいゆえ、長らく宝石には不向きとされてきました。そうした事情もあり、煌めきの割には入手しやすい価格です。

## A Wide Range of Colors from Orange to Green, Soft but Ideal for Pendants

Sphalerite is a gemstone that captivates viewers with its intense and overwhelming brilliance. This dazzling effect is due to its refractive index, comparable to that of diamonds, and its dispersion rate, which is four times greater than that of diamonds.

　When exposed to light, sphalerite sparkles intensely, with rainbow-colored flashes of light, known as "fire," appearing across its facets. However, with a Mohs hardness of only 3.5–4, sphalerite is relatively soft and brittle, making it historically unsuitable for use in jewelry.

　Because of these characteristics, despite its stunning brilliance, sphalerite remains relatively affordable and accessible.

## 亜鉛精製用の鉱石から
## ごく稀に見つかる宝石

　スファレライトは鉱物学上では、硫化亜鉛に属します。主として、亜鉛を精製するための工業用の鉱石として採掘されてきました。濃い褐色や黒色の原石がほとんどを占めますが、ごく稀にオレンジやイエロー、緑などの色合いを帯びた透明の原石が発見されることがあります。

　やわらかく、一方向に割れやすい性質から研磨することも困難であるものの、ごく一部の原石は宝石に加工することが可能だとわかりました。指輪にアレンジするとキズがつきやすく、もろいため、ペンダントなどに適しています。

　主な産出地は、スペイン、ブルガリア、フランス、ブラジルなどです。なかでも、スペイン産のイエロー系とブルガリア産のオレンジ系の石が質が高く美しいと評価を受けています。残念ながら、スファレライトの産出量は全般的に安定しているとはいいがたい状況です。

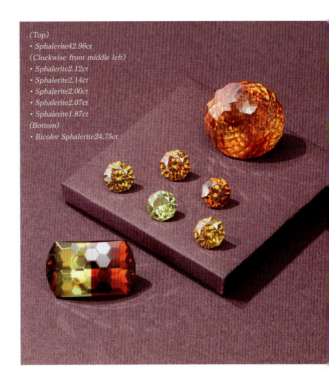

(Top)
- Sphalerite42.96ct
(Clockwise from middle left)
- Sphalerite2.12ct
- Sphalerite2.14ct
- Sphalerite2.00ct
- Sphalerite2.07ct
- Sphalerite1.87ct
(Bottom)
- Bicolor Sphalerite24.75ct

## A Rare Gemstone Found Among Zinc Ore

Mineralogically, sphalerite belongs to the zinc sulfide group and has primarily been mined as an industrial ore for zinc refinement. Most rough sphalerite is dark brown or black, but transparent crystals with orange, yellow, or green colors are found on extremely rare occasions.

Due to its softness and tendency to cleave in one direction, cutting and polishing sphalerite is challenging. However, a small number of rough stones can be processed into gemstones. Because of its fragility and susceptibility to scratches, it is better suited for pendants rather than rings.

The main sources of sphalerite include Spain, Bulgaria, France, and Brazil. Among them, yellow-toned stones from Spain and orange-toned stones from Bulgaria are particularly valued for their quality and beauty. Unfortunately, the overall supply of sphalerite remains inconsistent.

## Color variations

真っ赤からオレンジ、イエロー、淡い黄色、やや緑がかったものまで多彩。選択する際の大きなポイントは、輝きの強さ。

A wide variety of colors, from deep red to orange, yellow, pale yellow, and slightly greenish tones. The key factor in selection is the strength of its brilliance.

## Map of Sphalerite-Producing Countries

※おもな産出国や地域を記載しています
※Main producing countries and regions

## 純粋無垢を思わせる
## ライラックピンクの輝き

清楚で可憐、透明感のあるライラックピンクが印象的なクンツァイト。紫がかったピンクは、内包される酸化マンガンの影響で生まれます。

発見されたのは1902年、アメリカのカリフォルニア州でのことでした。当初はトルマリンと誤認されましたが、リチウムを主成分とする石と判明。ティファニーの伝説的鑑定士のクンツ博士に敬意を表し、その名を冠することになりました。

ブラジル、アフガニスタンで安定した産出が続き、良質なものの価格は上がっていますが、比較的大粒を手に入れやすい宝石です。

### The Lilac Pink Radiance That Evokes Pure Innocence

Kunzite is a gemstone known for its pure, delicate, and transparent lilac-pink color. Its purplish pink color is caused by the presence of manganese oxide contained within the stone.

Discovered in 1902 in California, USA, kunzite was initially mistaken for tourmaline but was later identified as a lithium-based mineral. It was named in honor of Dr. George Frederick Kunz, the legendary gemologist at Tiffany & Co.

Kunzite is still steadily mined in Brazil and Afghanistan. Although the price of high-quality stones has been rising, it remains relatively affordable, even for larger-sized gems.

Semi-Precious Stone

# Kunzite

クンツァイト

(Clockwise from the left)
- Pt Pendant_Kunzite8.22ct,D0.04ct
- Pt Pendant_Kunzite35.92ct,D3.11ct
- YG Ring_Kunzite3.98ct,D0.56ct

### Map of Kunzite-Producing Countries

※おもな産出国や地域を記載しています
※Main producing countries and regions

Semi-Precious Stone

# Morganite

モルガナイト

## 大粒のジュエリーで堪能したい
## 淡いピンクの光の乱舞

モルガナイトは鉱物学ではベリルに属し、内包される微量のマンガンにより淡いピンク色が生まれます。ブリリアントカットにすると華やかなピンクの光の乱舞が見られます。

1911年にマダガスカルで発見され、現在も金融機関に名が残るJ.P.モルガンにちなみ、モルガナイトと命名されました。財閥の創業者にして宝石コレクターとしても名高い人物だったためです。

### Savor the Dance of Pale Pink Light in Large Gemstones

Morganite belongs to the beryl family, with its pale pink color resulting from trace amounts of manganese. When cut in a brilliant style, morganite showcases a lively dance of pink light.

Discovered in Madagascar in 1911, it was named "morganite" after J.P. Morgan, a prominent financier and renowned gemstone collector, whose name remains linked to financial institutions.

*(From top to bottom)*
- PG Ring_Morganite2.31ct,D0.90ct
- PG Pendant_Morganite27.99ct, Scapolite1.09ct,D0.08ct
- WG Pendant_Morganite5.17ct,D0.235ct
- Pt Pendant_Morganite2.19ct,D0.46ct

## Map of Morganite-Producing Countries

※おもな産出国や地域を記載しています
※Main producing countries and regions

(From top left)
• Gray Spinel1.13ct
• Purple Spinel11.74ct
(From the middle left)
• Pt Ring_Pink Spinel1.18ct,D0.753ct
• Blue Spinel2.21ct
• WG Pendant_Violet Spinel2.09ct,D0.14ct
(From the top of the bottom row)
• YG Ring_Red Spinel1.765ct,D0.07ct
• YG Ring_Red Spinel1.03ct,D0.84ct

Semi-Precious Stone

# Spinel

スピネル

## ルビー、サファイアと見紛う 気高い風格、美に満ちた宝石

　深い赤や青の人気が高いスピネルには、長らくルビー、サファイアと混同されてきた歴史があります。イギリス王室の第一公式王冠の正面に据えられた有名な「黒太子のルビー」も、実は赤いスピネルだと明らかになりました。スピネルがいかに美しく輝く宝石であるかを物語っています。

　赤、青のほかに、ピンク、赤紫、緑、オレンジ、グレーなどスピネルには豊富な色相があり、色は濃いほど高く評価されます。非常に稀少価値が高いのがミャンマー産のコバルトブルー。赤いスピネルについてもミャンマー産は人気です。

### A Gemstone of Noble Elegance and Beauty That Rivals Rubies and Sapphires

Spinel, popular for its deep red and blue colors, has a long history of being mistaken for ruby and sapphire. One of the most famous examples is the "Black Prince's Ruby," prominently set in the front of the British Imperial State Crown, which was later identified as a red spinel. This highlights the remarkable brilliance and beauty of spinel.

In addition to red and blue, spinel comes in a variety of colors, including pink, reddish-purple, green, orange, and gray. The deeper the color, the more valuable it is. Among the rarest is cobalt blue spinel from Myanmar, a region also celebrated for its exceptional red spinel.

### Map of Spinel-Producing Countries

※おもな産出国や地域を記載しています
※Main producing countries and regions

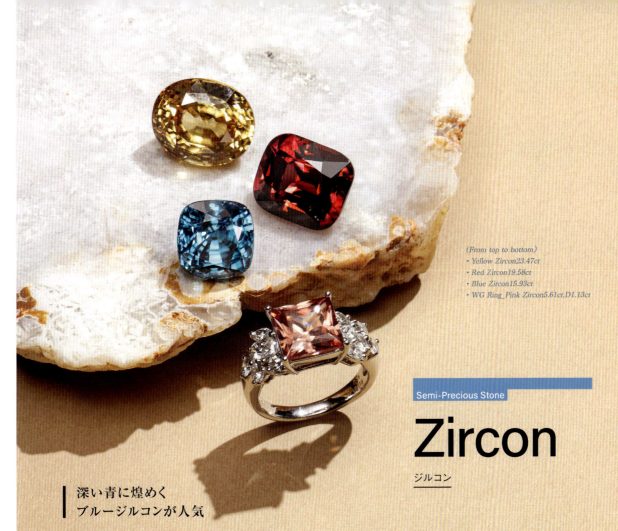

(From top to bottom)
- Yellow Zircon 23.47ct
- Red Zircon 19.58ct
- Blue Zircon 15.93ct
- WG Ring_Pink Zircon 5.61ct, D1.13ct

Semi-Precious Stone

# Zircon

ジルコン

## 深い青に煌めく
## ブルージルコンが人気

屈折率が非常に高く、無色ではダイヤモンドに似た煌めきを見せるジルコン。深い青、赤褐色、黄褐色、橙色、緑など多彩な色みがあります。

44億年前に生成された原石もあり、スリランカでは2000年前から採掘されていたといわれるほど、ジルコンには長い歴史があります。

ブルージルコンは1920年から市場に流通し始めた新顔ですが、その強い輝きが人気です。主にカンボジアで産出されて加熱処理され、そのごく一部が美しい青になります。ミャンマー産のレッドジルコンはさらに稀少性の高い石です。

## The Sparkling Deep Blue of Blue Zircon is Highly Coveted

Zircon, known for its exceptionally high refractive index, exhibits a diamond-like brilliance when colorless. It comes in a wide variety of colors, including deep blue, reddish-brown, yellow-brown, orange, and green.

Some zircon crystals were formed as long as 4.4 billion years ago, and it is said that mining in Sri Lanka began around 2,000 years ago, reflecting its long history.

Blue zircon, a relative newcomer to the market since the 1920s, is admired for its intense brilliance. It is primarily mined in Cambodia, where heat treatment produces its striking blue color in only a small fraction of the stones. Red zircon from Myanmar is even rarer.

## Map of Zircon-Producing Countries

※おもな産出国や地域を記載しています
※Main producing countries and regions

147

# Rare
# Stones

レアストーン

地球上に存在する鉱物は、5,200種類以上に上るといわれます。そのなかで、宝石と呼べる石がどれだけあるかというと、約200種と見られています。そんなに種類が多いのかと驚く人は多いでしょう。宝石の世界は、一般に考えられているより実はずっと多様です。

レアストーンとは、これまで流通や採掘、研磨技術などの問題から、市場に出回ることが少なかった宝石です。近年は、国内の市場でも出会える機会が拡がりました。ここでは、一般的には知名度はまだ高くないものの、まるで宇宙からの贈り物といえる美しい色石をご紹介します。

It is estimated that more than 5,200 types of minerals exist on Earth. Among them, only about 200 are considered gemstones. Many may be surprised by this number, as the world of gemstones is far more diverse than commonly thought.

"Rare stones" are gemstones that have rarely appeared on the market due to factors such as limited distribution, mining challenges, or cutting and polishing difficulties. In recent years, however, opportunities to encounter them have increased, even in domestic markets. Here, we introduce beautiful colored stones that, though not yet widely known, can be described as true gifts from the cosmos.

*(Clockwise from top left)*
- *Pt Pendant_Pallasite Peridot0.254ct,D0.10ct*
- *Pt /YG Ring_Pallasite Peridot0.777ct,D0.17ct*
- *Pallasite Peridot0.971ct*
- *Pallasite Peridot0.281ct*

Rare Stone

# Pallasite Peridot

パラサイトペリドット

宇宙からの贈り物

*The Gift from the Universe*

## 隕石から発見される　宇宙生まれのペリドット

　隕石から採れたペリドットがパラサイトペリドットです。鉄とケイ酸塩鉱物でできた石鉄隕石のわずか1％ほどから見つかり、18世紀にドイツの博物学者の名前にちなみ命名されました。

　地球起源のペリドットと比べ褐色の内包物が多く、イエローや褐色の色みがやや強く見える傾向があります。ほとんどがごく小粒の石で、宇宙から地球の大気圏突入には大きな圧力がかかるため、劈開(へきかい)が多く見られます。

　石鉄隕石が硬いため、これまで研磨が難しく宝石質のものを取り出すのが困難でしたが、近年研磨技術の向上によって宝石質のものが出回るようになりました。0.1カラットを超えるものは少なく0.3カラット以上でも稀少で、1カラット以上は非常に高価です。隕石由来のため、当然鉱山は存在せず、見つかるかどうかは運次第の宝石です。

## Peridot from Space: Found in Meteorites

Pallasite peridot is peridot from meteorites, found in only about 1% of stony-iron meteorites, which consist of iron and silicate minerals. The name "pallasite" was given in the 18th century after a German naturalist.

　Compared to Earth-origin peridot, pallasite peridot has more brownish inclusions and tends to show stronger yellow or brown tones. Most stones are very small, and due to the intense pressure meteorites face when entering Earth's atmosphere, cleavage is common.

　Stony-iron meteorites are extremely hard, making it difficult to extract gem-quality peridot. However, advances in cutting and polishing techniques have made these stones more available. Still, those over 0.1 carats are uncommon, and over 0.3 carats are rare. Specimens exceeding 1 carat are extremely rare and highly valuable. Since these gems come from meteorites, no mines exist—finding one is purely a matter of luck.

(Clockwise from top left)
- WG Pendant_Stella Esperanza15.46ct,D0.665ct
- YG Pendant_Stella Esperanza13.46ct, D0.58ct
- WG Pendant_Stella Esperanza3.32ct, D0.37ct
- Stella Esperanza30.89ct

# Stella Esperanza

ステラエスペランサ

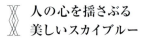 人の心を揺さぶる
美しいスカイブルー

　半透明で爽やかな空のようなブルーが目を引くステラエスペランサ。鉱物名はヘミモルファイト（異極鉱）といい、結晶の端が一方は尖り、もう一方は平面というように形が異なる特徴があります。無色、青、緑、黄色、茶色などのヘミモルファイトは、古来、世界各地で採掘されてきました。

　美しく蛍光するブルーの石が見つかったのは、2005年頃のこと。パライバトルマリンの産出で名高いブラジルのパライバ州パレーリャス鉱山近くでのことでした。高い価値を確信したブラジル人オーナーは、一括販売してくれる宝石業者があらわれるまで手元で管理を続けることにしました。

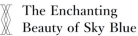 The Enchanting
Beauty of Sky Blue

Stella Esperanza captivates with its translucent, refreshing sky-blue color. Its mineral name, hemimorphite, refers to a crystal with a unique asymmetric structure—one end terminating in a sharp tip, the other in a flat surface. Found in various colors, including colorless, blue, green, yellow, and brown, hemimorphite has been mined worldwide since ancient times.

　The discovery of its beautifully fluorescent blue variety dates back to around 2005. It was found near the famed Parelhas mines in Paraíba state, Brazil, known for Paraiba tourmalines. Recognizing its value, the Brazilian owner kept it in his possession until a suitable gem dealer appeared to handle a large-scale sale.

Rare Stone

## 「希望の星」と命名され 2010年に日本デビュー

そうして巡り合ったのが、ギンザベルエトワールの創業者、岡本憲将氏でした。オーナーから命名を依頼された岡本氏は、「希望の星」を意味するステラエスペランサと名付け、2010年、日本の宝石市場に披露することとなりました。

実は、スカイブルーの原石は他地域でもわずかに産出され、「悪霊を祓う石」として崇められた歴史がありました。半透明ながら青く透き通るような宝石質の原石は極端なまでに少ないため、その存在がほとんど知られていなかったのです。今日でもブラジルのほか、アフリカのコンゴが産出地ではありますが、ほとんど産出されておらず、稀少価値は高まる一方です。

## Star of Hope: Debuting in Japan in 2010

It was then that Mr. Kensho Okamoto, founder of Ginza Belle Etoile, became involved. Entrusted with naming the gemstone, he chose "Stella Esperanza," meaning "Star of Hope." In 2010, it was introduced to the Japanese jewelry market.

Interestingly, rough sky-blue stones have been found in small quantities elsewhere and were once revered as "stones that ward off evil spirits." However, gem-quality translucent blue specimens are extremely rare, making them largely unknown. Today, aside from Brazil, the Democratic Republic of the Congo is also a source, but production remains minimal, and their rarity continues to increase.

(From left to right)
- Pt Pendant_Stella Esperanza3.13ct,D0.36ct
- WG Pendant_Stella Esperanza14.70ct,D11.74ct
- Pt Earrings_Stella Esperanza3.95ct,D1.335ct, Stella Esperanza3.07ct,D1.335ct
- Pt Pendant_Stella Esperanza4.75ct,Pallasite Peridot0.58ct,D0.60ct

希望を映すスカイブルー
*Sky Blue Reflecting Hope*

# Hauynite
アウイナイト

― 小粒でも鮮烈な美しさ
*Tiny but Strikingly Beautiful*

(Clockwise from top left)
- Pt Ring_Hauynite0.29ct,D0.87ct
- Pt Ring_Hauynite0.43ct,D0.64ct
- WG Pendant_Hauynite0.32ct,D0.471ct
- Pt Ring_Hauynite0.79ct,D1.2ct

超がつくほどの稀少石で、ほとんどが小粒で硬度も低いながら、コバルトブルーの鮮烈な輝きが見る人を虜にし、非常に高い価値があります。

現在の主な産出地は、ドイツ中西部のアイフェル地方です。ただし、国立公園内にあるため大規模な採掘を行うことはかないません。数年前まで公園の整備に伴い、ある程度まとまった産出がありましたが、今後、その可能性は低いといえます。

This exceptionally rare gemstone mesmerizes with its vivid cobalt-blue brilliance. Though small and relatively soft, its striking beauty and rarity make it highly valuable.

Today, its primary source is the Eifel region in central-western Germany. However, as the deposits lie within a national park, large-scale mining is not permitted. Until a few years ago, some extraction occurred during park maintenance, but future mining prospects remain slim.

# Green Hauynite
グリーンアウイナイト

― 宝石質のものはレア
*Rare in Gem-Quality*

青いアウイナイトの鮮やかな煌めきと異なり、落ち着いた印象を醸すグリーンアウイナイト。明るく澄んだ緑色は、紫外線のもとでピンクに蛍光するという稀有な特徴があります。

レアストーンの仲間入りをしたのは、アフガニスタンで発見された最近のこと。小粒がほとんどで、内包物があっても肉眼で見た美しさを損ねなければさほど問題ないでしょう。

(Clockwise from top left)
- Pt Pendant_Green Hauynite0.34ct,D0.08ct
- Pt Pendant_Green Hauynite0.4ct,D0.4ct
- Green Hauynite0.43ct

Unlike the vivid brilliance of blue hauyne, green hauyne has a more subdued elegance. Its bright, clear green color exhibits a rare phenomenon—it fluoresces pink under ultraviolet light.

This gemstone was only recently recognized as a rare stone after its discovery in Afghanistan. Most specimens are small, and inclusions are generally not an issue as long as they do not affect its beauty to the naked eye.

# Rare Stone

## Hyalite
ハイアライト

### ミステリアスに変貌
### A Mysterious Transformation

ハイアライトは、ハイアライトオパールとも呼ばれ、遊色はしないけれど、オパールの一種です。ブラックライトを当てると蛍光するものもあります。自然界のウランを取り込んだことにより起こる変貌です。淡い青、ごく薄い緑などの石が、突如として鮮やかに蛍光することは大きな魅力。「ミステリーストーン」の呼び名もあります。

主な産出地はメキシコ、スペインなどです。

Hyalite, also known as hyalite opal, is a type of opal that lacks play-of-color. However, some specimens fluoresce vividly under black light due to trace amounts of natural uranium. Stones in pale blue or very light green tones suddenly glow with striking fluorescence, enhancing their mystique and earning them the nickname "Mystery Stone."

The primary sources of hyalite are Mexico and Spain.

*(From left to right)*
- Hyalite8.65ct
- YG Ring_ Hyalite3.92ct,D1.03ct

**UVライトで変化 / Changes under UV light**

---

## Scapolite
スキャポライト

### 劇的に蛍光する石
### A Dramatically Fluorescent Stone

紫色、黄色、無色透明の石が多くを占め、ほかにピンクや褐色などの色もあるスキャポライト。

近年になり、UVライトを当てると強い蛍光色を発するスキャポライトが市場に登場し、注目されています。特にタンザニアのメレラニ鉱山で採れたスキャポライトには、変色するものが多い傾向があるといわれます。変色しなくても、黄色や紫など美しい色合いのものも人気があります。

Scapolite is commonly found in shades of purple, yellow, and colorless transparency, with occasional variations in pink and brown.

In recent years, scapolite that fluoresces vividly under UV light has gained attention in the market. Specimens from the Merelani Hills in Tanzania are particularly known for their tendency to change color. Even without this trait, beautifully colored stones in yellow or purple remain sought after.

*(Clockwise from top left)*
- Scapolite21.71ct
- Scapolite3.74ct
- Scapolite1.92ct
- Scapolite3.69ct

**UVライトで変化 / Changes under UV light**

(From left to right)
· Pt Pendant_Cassiterite4.04ct,D0.44ct
· Cassiterite3.10ct
· Cassiterite3.991ct

# Cassiterite

キャシテライト

極上の煌めきの魅力

*The Allure of Exquisite Brilliance*

和名の錫鉱石（すずいし）からわかる通り、原石は錫を採取する鉱石として用いられます。原石は通常、黒や濃い褐色で、稀に宝石質のキャシテライトが産出されます。色みは淡いイエローから褐色まであり、これは鉄分の影響によるものです。

分散率はダイヤモンドをしのぐほどで、美しい煌めきを楽しめます。ブラウンダイヤモンドを思わせるファイアが見られる石もあります。

Rough cassiterite is a tin ore used for tin extraction. It is usually black or dark brown, but gem-quality specimens are occasionally found. Its color varies from pale yellow to brown due to iron content.

With a dispersion rate exceeding that of diamonds, cassiterite boasts exceptional brilliance. Some stones display fire reminiscent of brown diamonds, adding to their rarity and allure.

アメリカのオレゴン州で1910年代に発見。無色から赤、赤褐色、緑色、黄色など幅広い色相があり、ひとつの石に複数の石が混ざり合っているのも魅力的です。鉱物学上は長石の一種であるラブラドライトであり、中に入り込んだ銅の結晶片により輝きを放ちます。コマーシャルネームなので、鑑別書ではラブラドライトの名称が用いられます。鉱山は州内に複数ありますが、産出はごく稀です。

Discovered in Oregon, USA, in the 1910s, this gemstone displays a broad spectrum of colors, from colorless to red, reddish-brown, green, and yellow. One of its most captivating features is how multiple colors blend within a single stone. Mineralogically, it is a variety of feldspar known as labradorite, with its brilliance stemming from tiny copper inclusions. Though commonly marketed under the commercial name "Oregon Sunstone," gemological certificates classify it as labradorite. While multiple mines exist within the state, production is exceptionally rare, adding to its exclusivity and value.

# Oregon Sunstone

オレゴンサンストーン

(Clockwise from the left)
· Oregon Sunstone12.46ct
· Pt Ring_Oregon Sunstone4.72ct
· Oregon Sunstone1.96ct

米オレゴン州生まれ

*Originating from Oregon, USA*

Rare Stone

約2000年前の大噴火を起こしたイタリアのヴェスビオ火山。その山中から1795年に発見されました。鉱物名は「ヴェスビアナイト」。ケニア、ロシア、アメリカなどでも産出されます。

色相が豊かで、人気が高いのは独特のやや褐色みのある緑。濃い茶色で美しく輝く石もあります。透明度の高いものは稀少で、半透明のものは多くがカボションカットされています。

Mount Vesuvius in Italy, famous for its massive eruption nearly 2,000 years ago, was the site of vesuvianite's discovery in 1795. Named after the volcano, this mineral is also called "idocrase" in the gemstone market. It is sourced in Kenya, Russia, and the United States.

Known for its rich color variations, the most sought-after specimens feature a distinctive green with a slight brownish tint. Some also exhibit a deep brown brilliance. Transparent vesuvianite is rare, while semi-transparent stones are more common and often cut into cabochons to enhance their beauty.

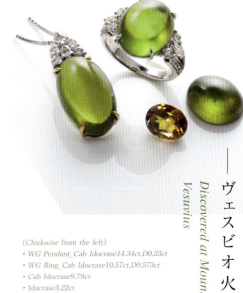

*Discovered at Mount Vesuvius* ― ヴェスビオ火山で発見

(Clockwise from the left)
- WG Pendant_Cab Idocrase14.34ct,D0.33ct
- WG Ring_Cab Idocrase10.57ct,D0.573ct
- Cab Idocrase9.79ct
- Idocrase3.22ct

# Idocrase

アイドクレース

# Kyanite

カイヤナイト

(Clockwise from the left)
- Kyanite5.59ct
- Kyanite5.97ct
- Kyanite22.33ct

*A Calm Elegance in Ultramarine* ― 群青の落ち着いた佇まい

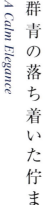

カイヤナイトの語源は、ギリシャ語で群青色を意味する「kyanos」。和名は「藍晶石（らんしょうせき）」で、やはり深みある青色をあらわしています。ブルーサファイアと見紛うような落ち着いた印象的な色です。

もともと内包物が多く、色味もムラがあるなど、透明感が高く美しい石は非常にレア。アメリカ、ブラジル、ネパールで産出されますが、鉱山が小規模であるため市場への供給が不安定です。

The name "kyanite" comes from the Greek word *kyanos*, meaning "deep blue." With its serene and striking color, kyanite is often mistaken for blue sapphire.

Kyanite naturally contains many inclusions, and its color can be uneven, making highly transparent and beautiful stones exceptionally rare. While found in the United States, Brazil, and Nepal, deposits are small, resulting in an unstable market supply.

155

## Apatite
アパタイト

### 注目のパライバカラー
*The Mesmerizing Paraiba Color*

(From left to right)
- Pt/YG Pendant_Apatite0.78ct,D0.44ct
- Pt Pendant_Apatite5.98ct,D0.28ct
- WG Pendant_Apatite7.74ct,D0.36ct
- WG Pendant_Apatite4.25ct,D0.41ct

鉱物学ではリン酸塩鉱物に属し、内包する金属元素によって青、緑、黄色、黄緑色、褐色などの色が生まれます。

ごく稀に、パライバトルマリンを思わせるネオンブルーの石が見つかります。これはブラジル・パライバ州バターリャ付近のパライバトルマリンの鉱山近くで採れるもの。マダガスカルでも産出されますが、パライバカラーの石はありません。

Apatite is classified as a phosphate mineral. Its color varies depending on the metallic elements it contains, ranging from blue and green to yellow, yellow-green, and brown.

On rare occasions, neon blue stones reminiscent of Paraiba tourmaline are found. These exceptional gems are mined near the Paraiba tourmaline deposits in Batalha, Paraíba state, Brazil. While Madagascar also produces apatite, it does not yield stones in the coveted Paraiba blue.

## Benitoite
ベニトアイト

### アメリカ「三大稀少石」
*One of America's Three Rare Gemstones*

(Clockwise from the top)
- Pt Ring_Benitoite1.95ct,D1.67ct
- Pt Pendant_Benitoite1.42ct,D0.26ct
- Pt Ring_Benitoite0.52ct,D0.10ct

カリフォルニア州のサンベニトという地域で1906年に発見され、産出地もこの1カ所だけで、鉱物名がそのまま宝石名としても使われています。

カリフォルニア州の公式の石にして、アメリカの「三大稀少石」にも指定。残念ながら産出はすでに途絶え、発見されてから100年の間に採れた原石は合計2400カラットにすぎず、その価値は上昇し続けています。

Discovered in 1906 in San Benito County, California, benitoite is named after its sole known source. Both the mineral and gemstone share the same name, an uncommon trait in the gem world.

Recognized as California's official state gem, benitoite is also designated as one of America's three rarest gemstones. However, production has ceased, and in over a century, only 2,400 carats of rough stones have been mined, driving its value ever higher.

Rare Stone

青、緑、赤、黄色など豊富な色があるフローライト。サファイアやルビー、エメラルドの代用品とされた時代もありました。

紫外線を当てると蛍光色に発色し、「蛍石(ほたるいし)」とも呼ばれます。ブラジル産の多色性があるフローライトは大変美しく、超稀少です。

硬度が4と軟らかく、特定の方向に割れやすい性質があり、取り扱いには注意が必要です

Fluorite occurs in a wide range of colors, including blue, green, red, and yellow. In the past, it was even used as a substitute for sapphire, ruby, and emerald.

Under ultraviolet light, fluorite glows in fluorescent colors, earning it the name "fluorescent stone." Particularly stunning are the pleochroic fluorites from Brazil, which are exceptionally rare and highly prized.

With a Mohs hardness of 4, fluorite is relatively soft and prone to cleavage along specific planes, requiring careful handling.

(Clockwise from the top)
・Fluorite19.26ct
・Fluorite20.65ct
・Fluorite10.48ct

# Fluorite
フローライト

――紫外線で蛍光する「蛍石」
*Fluorite: A Stone That Glows under UV Light*

# Vayrynenite
ヴェイリネナイト

(Clockwise from the top)
・Vayrynenite0.25ct
・Vayrynenite0.13ct
・Vayrynenite0.18ct

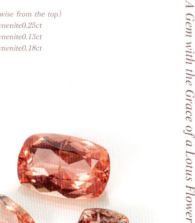

――蓮のような美しい色
*A Gem with the Grace of a Lotus Flower*

蓮の花を思わせる色がパパラチアサファイアにたとえられるヴェイリネナイト。オレンジからピンクの鮮やかな色みが、見る人の心を奪います。

20世紀半ばにフィンランドで発見され、アメリカ、中国など各地で稀に産出されてきました。その後、パキスタン、アフガニスタンで宝石質の石が見つかりましたが、採れる量は限定的。大粒の石は産出されず、市場に出る石も限られています。

Vayrynenite, often likened to padparadscha sapphire for its resemblance to the lotus flower, captivates with its vivid orange-to-pink color. Its striking colors leave a lasting impression.

Discovered in Finland in the mid-20th century, this rare gemstone has since been sporadically found in the United States, China, and other regions. Later, gem-quality specimens were uncovered in Pakistan and Afghanistan, though production remains extremely limited. Large stones are never found, and only a small number reach the market.

# 宝石の4つの価値
## The 4 Values of Gemstones

宝石の主な価値は4つあります。財産、美しさ、装飾、エネルギーとしての価値です。それぞれについて見ていきましょう。

The main values of gemstones are four: assets, beauty, adornment, and energy. Let's explore each one.

文・岡本敬人
株式会社ベル・エトワール代表取締役

Text: Takahito Okamoto
President & CEO of
Belle Etoile Co.,Ltd.

### 1
Gemstones as Assets

## 財産として

…

**種類と質、大きさが重要**

　宝石の財産としての価値は、ユダヤの人々の歴史を振り返るとよくわかります。イスラエル建国まで国をもたず、各地に離散していた彼らは、追害から逃れる際の資金として宝石を用いました。世界のどこでも価値が認められていて換金でき、いざという時には容易に持ち運べる宝石を日頃から財産として蓄えていたのです。

　日本は空前の投資ブームといわれますが、その対象は株式や不動産がほとんど。宝石を資産と捉える人はさほど多くありません。理解や認識の不足はまだまだ解消されていないといえます。

　財産的な価値を重視してジュエリーを購入する際、重要なのは中石と呼ばれるメインの宝石です。中石の周囲を華やかに飾る小さなダイヤモンドではなく、中石の種類と質、そして大きさによって財産価値は決定づけられます。よく見極めて適正な価格で購入すれば、将来的に価値が極端に下がるようなことはないでしょう。

　では、どんな種類の宝石を選んだら財産としての価値が高いのでしょうか。一般的に、ルビー、サファイア、エメラルド、ダイヤモンドなど昔からメジャーな石は、安定して高い水準の価値をもちます。

　一方、比較的新しく発見された宝石でも、急

激に人気が上昇し、稀少価値が高まったことから、財産的に非常に高く評価されるものもあります。

その最たる例がパライバトルマリンです。鮮烈なネオンブルーが世界的に人気を博しましたが、産地が限られるうえ良質なものがほとんど採れなくなり、稀少性がますます高まりました。ブラジル産の高品質なものは、20〜30年の間に数倍から、ものによっては数百倍にまで高騰しています。

宝石の中で一番価値が高いのは、ダイヤモンドだと思っている方も多いかもしれません。もちろん質の高いダイヤモンドは価値も高く財産性もありますが、実は多くの色石のほうが産出量が少なく、稀少価値の高いものが多いのも事実です。産出が激減したり、止まったことから、価格が高騰している色石も多く、財産として考えるなら、産出状況とその人気は注目すべきポイントになるでしょう。

宝石の質については、色、輝き、内包物のバランスが重要です。次ページの価値基準表を参考にしてください。

大きさについては、石の種類により異なりますが、財産的価値を求めて購入する場合、1カラット以上を目安にするといいでしょう。

## Type, Quality, and Size Matter

The historical experience of the Jewish people clearly illustrates the value of gemstones as assets. Until the establishment of Israel, they had no nation of their own and were scattered across various regions. During times of persecution, they used gemstones as financial resources. Recognized worldwide for their value, easily converted into cash, and highly portable, gemstones were accumulated as a form of wealth.

Japan is experiencing an unprecedented investment boom, but the focus is mostly on stocks and real estate. Few people consider gemstones as assets, and awareness remains low.

When purchasing jewelry for its asset value, the most important factor is the center stone, the main gemstone. Unlike small diamonds that simply decorate the setting, the asset value depends on the type, quality, and size of the center stone. If carefully chosen and purchased at a fair price, its value is unlikely to decline significantly over time.

So, which gemstones can have strong asset value?

Generally, well-established gemstones such as rubies, sapphires, emeralds, and diamonds maintain stable, high value.

However, some gemstones have gained significant asset value despite being discovered relatively recently. This is due to their rising popularity and increasing rarity. A prime example is Paraiba tourmaline. Its vivid neon blue color has gained worldwide popularity, but its limited sources and the decreasing availability of high-quality specimens have made it increasingly rare. High-quality Paraiba tourmalines from Brazil have surged in price, increasing several times—or even hundreds of times—over the past 20 to 30 years.

Many people may believe that diamonds are the most valuable gemstones. While high-quality diamonds do hold significant value and are considered assets, many colored gemstones are rarer due to their lower production volumes, making them highly valuable as well. In fact, many colored gemstones are no longer mined or are hardly being mined, leading to soaring prices. Considering production trends and popularity as key factors in assessing their asset value is worthwhile.

A gemstone's quality depends on the balance of color, brilliance, and inclusions. Refer to the value standards table on the next page for details.

As for size, the right choice depends on the type of gemstone. However, for investment purposes, at least one carat is a good guide.

# 宝石の4つの価値 | The 4 Values of Gemstones

## 価値ある宝石の選び方
### How to Choose Valuable Gemstones

　価値の判断ポイントは、色、内包物、輝きの3つ。色は濃くなるにつれ点数が上がり、最高色を過ぎて黒ずむにつれ下がります（下図参照）。色は最も重要であるため200点満点とします。内包物は、量や入り方に応じて100点満点で評価。輝きも最高を100点として評価します。これら3つの点数を足して、総合点を出します。

Gemstones are evaluated based on three factors: color, inclusions, and brilliance.
　Color is the most important factor, so it is given a maximum of 200 points. The score increases as the color becomes deeper, reaching its highest point at the best shade. However, if the color becomes too dark or blackish, the score decreases (see diagram below).
　Inclusions are graded out of 100 points, with the score depending on their amount and placement. Brilliance is also evaluated on a 100-point scale, with the highest level receiving full marks. The total score is determined by summing these values.

### 産地による色の違いとその評価 ［ルビーの場合］
Color Variations by Orign and Value (For Ruby)

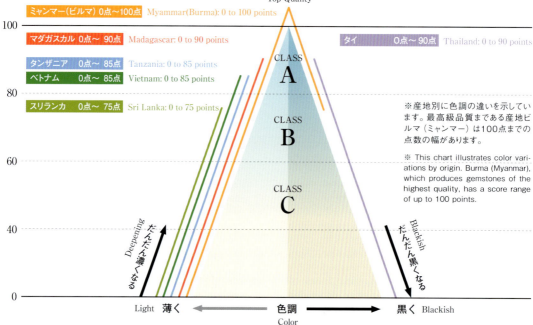

### 一般の色石採点基準表　Standard Grading Chart for Colored Gemstones

| 基準 Standard | | CLASS | CLASS A | CLASS B | CLASS C |
|---|---|---|---|---|---|
| 総合点（400点満点） | | Total Score | 320 or more | 240 or more | 160 or more |
| 項目 Entry | 色（200点満点） | Color (200 points) | 160 or more | 120 or more | 80 or more |
| | 内包物（インクルージョン）（100点満点） | Inclusion (100 points) | 80 or more | 60 or more | 40 or more |
| | 輝き（テリ）（100点満点） | Brilliance (100 points) | 80 or more | 60 or more | 40 or more |

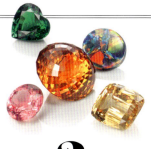

## 2

Gemstones as Beauty

# 美しさとして

...

**宝石の色と輝きを観賞**

　2つ目の価値は美しさ。悠久なる地球の歩みのなかで育まれた宝石の美しさは、見飽きることがありません。美しい色、まばゆい輝きの宝石との出会いは、感動を与えてくれます。手のひらにのせ、その宝石が生み出す美の世界を観賞しているだけで、心が癒され、満ち足りてくるでしょう。

　手に取ってさまざまな角度から眺め、光を変えてみるのもいいでしょう。UVライトなどを当てると色が大きく変わる石もあります。

　美しさを楽しむ宝石選びで重視されるのは、色と輝き。眺めていると心がときめき、元気になる、癒される宝石を選んでください。宝石は人生に「楽しみ」という大きな価値を与えてくれます。

### Appreciating the Color and Brilliance of Gemstones

Another key value is aesthetic appeal. The beauty of gemstones, formed over the vast span of Earth's history, is timeless and endlessly captivating. Their stunning colors and dazzling brilliance can leave a lasting impression. Simply holding a gemstone in your hand and admiring its beauty can calm your heart and fill you with contentment.

　Try viewing the gemstone from different angles and under various lighting conditions. Some stones display dramatic color changes under UV light.

　When choosing a gemstone for its beauty, focus on color and brilliance. Select one that makes your heart flutter, lifts your spirits, and brings you comfort. Gemstones add the precious value of enjoyment to life.

## 3

Gemstones as Adornment

# 装飾として

...

**普段用かフォーマル用か考えて選ぶ**

　3つ目は装飾としての価値。美しく輝く宝石を身につけた時、私たちは高揚感を覚え、幸せな気持ちに浸ることができます。

　かつては宝石を身につけるのはフォーマルな場に限るといった固定観念もありましたが、現在は好みに合ったシンプルなデザインのジュエリーを普段から身に着ける人が増えています。せっかくのジュエリーを宝石箱に入れっぱなしにするのは、もったいないことです。

　普段使いにする場合は、硬度の高い宝石が合っています。軟らかい石の場合は、指輪よりもペンダントにするのがおすすめです。

### Select for Daily or Formal Use

The value of adornment cannot be forgotten. Wearing a beautiful, radiant gemstone can give you a sense of exhilaration and immerse you in happiness.

　In the past, gemstones were often seen only for formal occasions. However, more people today wear simple, stylish jewelry that suits their taste in daily life. Keeping your jewelry locked away in a box is a missed opportunity to enjoy its beauty.

　For everyday wear, hard gemstones are ideal. Softer stones are better suited for pendants rather than rings.

# 4

Gemstones as Energy

# エネルギーとして

## 古代から活用されていた宝石の力

　4つ目の価値は宝石がもつエネルギーです。

　宝石は地殻が形成されるなかで育まれました。エメラルドやルビーはおよそ30億年、ダイヤモンドはそれ以上の歳月にわたり地中でエネルギーを蓄え、人間に発見されるのを待っていたのです。

　人間は古代より宝石が何か特別な力を秘めていると感じていました。だからこそ、地中深くから掘り出し、さまざまな加工を施して身に着けてきたのでしょう。護符として珍重した歴史は、世界中に残されています。

　自然とともに生きていた時代には、宝石のエネルギーを感じる力も強かったのではないでしょうか。身を護り、良い方向へ導いてくれると信じ、宝石のエネルギーを活用していたのです。世界中の王や権力者、宗教指導者たちが必ず宝石を身につけていたのも、そのためです。

　ところが、時代が下がり、次第に人間が自然から離れて暮らすようになると、宝石の力はいつしか忘れ去られ、権力や富の象徴、単なる装飾と考えられるようになってしまいました。

　しかし近年になり、ホリスティックな観点から改めて宝石のエネルギーが注目を集めるようになっています。環境汚染、複雑な人間関係、デジタル社会など、数多くのストレスにさらされる生活のなかで、心身に不調を抱える人が増え、宝石の持つ癒しの力が見直されつつあるのです。

　宝石店を訪れ、気になる石を手に取った瞬間に「これは自分の石だ」と確信した経験がある人もいるのではないでしょうか。宝石のエネルギーを享受するためには、石と持つ人との相性がとても重要です。宝石は私たちの心と体を癒してくれる特別な力をもっています。自分に合った石、必要な石を持つことは人生を豊かにするためにも大切なことなのです。

## The Energy of Gemstones Harnessed Since Ancient Times

The fourth value is the energy that gemstones hold. Gemstones were formed as the Earth's crust took shape, nurtured over billions of years. Emeralds and rubies have spent approximately three billion years underground, accumulating energy, while diamonds have stored even more over an even longer period, waiting to be discovered by humans.

Since ancient times, people have believed that gemstones possess a special influence. This belief led them to extract gemstones from deep within the earth, shape them, and wear them. Across cultures, gemstones have been treasured as protective amulets.

In an era when people lived in harmony with nature, they may have been more attuned to the energy of gemstones. They believed gemstones could protect them and guide them in a positive direction, actively harnessing them. This is why kings, rulers, and religious leaders across the world always adorned themselves with gemstones.

However, as people became more distanced from nature, the significance of gemstones was gradually forgotten. They came to be seen merely as symbols of wealth and status or as decorative objects.

In recent years, however, the energy of gemstones has regained attention from a holistic perspective. In a world burdened by environmental pollution, complex human relationships, and the stress of digital society, more people are experiencing mental and physical exhaustion. As a result, the healing power of gemstones is being reexamined.

Have you ever picked up a gemstone and in-

宝石の4つの価値 | The 4 Values of Gemstones

## 科学的検証が進む宝石のエネルギー

宝石のエネルギーは、肩こり、腰痛、花粉症、頭痛、冷え性などの身体的な不調から、気持ちが落ち込む、やる気が出ない、イライラするといった精神的な不調まで、さまざまな症状を改善、緩和してくれます。私たちが毎日を楽しく健やかに生きるサポートをしてくれるのです。

「非科学的だ」「ただの迷信だろう」と懐疑的に捉えられるのはもったいないと、近年、宝石のエネルギーを科学的に検証し、解明する取り組みが進んでいます。厳密な条件下で科学的な実験が繰り返され、ただの迷信として片づけられない興味深い結果が明らかになってきました。

長い間忘れられていた宝石のエネルギーという価値が、科学に裏打ちされた形で、癒しを求める現代の人々に活用される時代が来ているのです。体の痛みや心身の不調が緩和した例も枚挙にいとまがありません。宝石の力は大きな可能性を秘めているのです。

stantly felt, "This is my stone"? To fully benefit from their energy, the connection between the stone and its owner is crucial. Gemstones possess a unique ability to heal both the mind and body. Finding the right stone—one that truly resonates with you—can bring greater balance and fulfillment to your life.

## Scientific Research on Gemstone Energy

The energy of gemstones is believed to help alleviate various physical ailments such as shoulder stiffness, lower back pain, hay fever, headaches, and cold sensitivity, as well as mental issues like low mood, lack of motivation, and irritability. Gemstones support our daily well-being, helping us live with greater joy and vitality.

While some may dismiss this as "unscientific" or "mere superstition," it would be unfortunate to overlook its potential. In recent years, efforts to scientifically examine and validate gemstone energy have gained momentum. Under controlled conditions, repeated experiments have revealed intriguing results that cannot simply be dismissed as superstition.

This long-overlooked value of gemstone energy is now being rediscovered and scientifically supported, offering healing potential to those seeking relief in modern times. Countless cases of reduced physical pain and improved mental well-being suggest that gemstones may hold immense potential for enhancing health and balance.

# 宝石エネルギーの伝道師・岡本憲将
## A Leading Voice in Gemstone Energy: Mr. Kensho Okamoto

　時代とともに忘れられていた宝石のエネルギーに着目し、現代に適した活用方法の基礎を体系化したのが、株式会社ベル・エトワールの前代表取締役・岡本憲将氏です。40年以上に渡り、宝石業界の第一線で活躍し、日本の宝石の流通革命と啓蒙に尽くした人物です。

　憲将氏が宝石のエネルギーに強い関心をもったきっかけは、自らの鼻炎や冷え性がルビーを身につけることで改善した経験でした。それまで古い文献でお守りとしての価値や効能などを目にしても半信半疑でしたが、自身や身近な人たちに宝石のヒーリングを試すなかで絶大な力があると確信するようになりました。20年以上の歳月をかけ、どの宝石にどの様な効果効能があるかを調べ、データを蓄積していったのです。

　さまざまな不調を抱える現代人にこそ宝石の力が必要との信念のもと、憲将氏は科学による客観的な検証の道を模索しました。2015年には、東北大学名誉教授・日本統合医療学会名誉理事長の故・仁田新一先生を委員長に迎え、多くの科学者、医師が参加する検証委員会を発足しました。

　残念なことに憲将氏は実験なかばに急逝しましたが、義父である憲将氏とともに実験に携わっていた現・代表取締役の岡本敬人氏（本書監修）が遺志を継ぎました。そして3年半をかけてさまざまな科学実験を重ね、宝石の力は科学的に証明され始めたのです。

**岡本憲将** Kensho Okamoto

株式会社ベル・エトワール・前代表取締役
Former President, Belle Etoile Co., Ltd.

1946年、栃木県生まれ。中央大学卒業後、1970年に宝石業界に参入。世界各地で独自の輸入ルートを開拓、自らも多数の宝石鉱山を所有。東京・銀座にて宝石店「ギンザ ベル・エトワール」を運営。『宝石の常識』シリーズをはじめ、宝石の正しい知識を啓蒙するための著書も多数。2017年逝去。

Born in 1946 in Tochigi Prefecture, Mr. Okamoto graduated from Chuo University and entered the jewelry industry in 1970. He developed exclusive import routes worldwide and owned multiple gemstone mines. He operated the jewelry store Ginza Belle Etoile in Tokyo's Ginza district.In addition to managing his business, he authored numerous books, including the *Basic Knowledge of Gemstones* series, to promote accurate understanding of gemstones. He passed away in 2017.

Mr. Kensho Okamoto, former President & CEO of Belle Etoile Co., Ltd., was a pioneer who rediscovered the long-forgotten energy of gemstones and systematized its modern applications. For over 40 years, he played a leading role in the gemstone industry, dedicating himself to revolutionizing Japan's gemstone distribution and raising public awareness of the significance of gemstones.

　Mr. Okamoto's deep interest in gemstone energy began with his own experience—his rhinitis and sensitivity to cold improved after wearing a ruby. Initially skeptical of historical texts that described gemstones' protective and beneficial effects, he became convinced of their healing potential through personal trials on himself and those around him. Over two decades, he meticulously studied the effects of various gemstones and compiled a substantial body of data.

　Believing that gemstones could provide relief to modern individuals struggling with various physical and mental ailments, Mr. Okamoto sought scientific validation. In 2015, he established a verification committee led by the late Dr. Shinichi Nitta, Honorary Professor at Tohoku University and Honorary Director of the Japanese Society of Integrated Medicine. The committee included numerous scientists and medical professionals.

　Unfortunately, Mr. Okamoto passed away before the completion of the experiments. However, his son-in-law, Mr. Takahito Okamoto, the current President & CEO of Belle Etoile Co., Ltd. and supervisor of this publication, carried on his legacy. Over three and a half years, extensive scientific studies were conducted, and the effects of gemstones began to gain scientific validation.

## ドクターと共に宝石のエネルギーを科学的に検証

### Scientific Analysis of Gemstone Energies with Medical Experts

**村山清之 先生**　Dr. Kiyoshi Murayama

日本橋むらやまクリニック前院長
順天堂大学医学部麻酔科　非常勤講師
日本麻酔科学会　麻酔科専門医
日本ペインクリニック学会　認定医

Former Director, Nihonbashi Murayama Clinic／Part-time Lecturer, Department of Anesthesiology, Juntendo University Faculty of Medicine／Board-Certified Anesthesiologist, Japanese Society of Anesthesiologists／Certified Pain Clinician, Japan Society of Pain Clinicians

岡本敬人氏と村山清之先生
Mr. Takahito Okamoto and Dr. Kiyoshi Murayama

　宝石のエネルギーが人間に及ぼす効果効能を科学的に計測して立証するべく、2016年から2019年にかけて、故・岡本憲将氏と岡本敬人氏は、東北大学名誉教授の仁田新一氏を代表とする多くの医師や科学者の方たちと共に「統合医療領域におけるJEWELLNESS効果の検証委員会」を立ち上げ、さまざまな実験を行ってきました。「ジュウェルネス（JEWELLNESS）」は「Jewel（宝石）」と「Wellness（心身の健康）」を合わせた憲将氏の造語で、多くの人が宝石のように光り輝く人生を送れるようにとの願いがこもっています。

　その実験のひとつが、臨床応用に向けてペインクリニックの元院長・村山清之先生と共に行った、宝石による施術前後の痛みの度合いをスコアリングする評価実験です。2022年からは「ジュウェルネス外来」としてギンザベルエトワールで月に1回の実験を続けています。

　「関節や筋肉の痛みが軽減したり、腕や足の可動域が広くなったり、鼻炎や咳などの症状が緩和したり、ジュウェルネスによる効果には驚かされ、大きな可能性を感じています」と村山先生。

　次ページでは、ジュウェルネス外来で村山先生と岡本敬人氏が行った実験結果をご紹介します。

From 2016 to 2019, the late Mr. Kensho Okamoto and Mr. Takahito Okamoto collaborated with a team of doctors and scientists led by Dr. Shinichi Nitta, an honorary professor at Tohoku University, to scientifically measure and verify the effects of gemstone energy on the human body. They established the "JEWELLNESS Effect Verification Committee in the Field of Integrative Medicine" and conducted various experiments.

　"JEWELLNESS" is a term coined by Mr. Kensho Okamoto, combining "Jewel" and "Wellness," embodying his wish for many people to lead radiant and fulfilling lives, like sparkling gemstones.

　One of their experiments was an evaluation study conducted in collaboration with Dr. Kiyoshi Murayama, former director of a pain clinic, to score the degree of pain before and after gemstone treatments for potential clinical applications. Since 2022, these experiments have continued monthly at Ginza Belle Etoile under the name "JEWELLNESS Clinic."

　"We have been astonished by the effects of JEWELLNESS, such as reduced joint and muscle pain, improved range of motion in arms and legs, and alleviation of symptoms like rhinitis and cough. This research holds great potential," says Dr. Murayama.

　The following page presents the scoring sheets from the experiments conducted at the JEWELLNESS Clinic by Dr. Murayama and Mr. Takahito Okamoto.

# ジュウェルネス外来での実験結果
Experimental Results from the JEWELLNESS Clinic

## Data 1　50代・女性　病名　左手指関節痛
Female, 50s - Diagnosis: **Left-Hand Finger Joint Pain**

| | |
|---|---|
| **特筆すべき症状、痛み**<br>Notable Symptoms or Pain | ● 動かしたとき、触ったときに痛い<br>● Pain on Movement or Touch |
| **使用した宝石**<br>Gemstones Used | ● ドラゴンガーネット<br>● Dragon Garnet |
| **ヒーリング前後の自覚症状の変化**<br>Changes in Perceived Symptoms Before and After Therapy | 重い痛み　Heavy Pain　　　　　　4 ➡ 0<br>触った時の痛み　Pain on Touch　　4 ➡ 0<br>引きつるような痛み　Tight, Pulling Pain　3 ➡ 0 |
| **その他の変化**<br>Other Changes | ● 2〜3週間続いた痛みが取れて、その後も効果が続いている<br>● A pain that lasted for 2-3 weeks has resolved, and the effects have continued since then. |

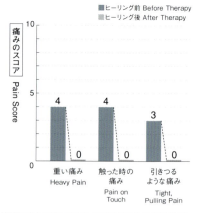

## Data 2　30代・男性　病名　全身打撲 (5日前のバイク事故よるもの)
Male, 30s - Diagnosis: **Whole-Body Bruises** (Caused by a Motorcycle Accident 5 Days Prior)

| | |
|---|---|
| **特筆すべき症状、痛み**<br>Notable Symptoms or Pain | ● 頸部痛（首から両肩にかけての痛み）<br>● 首が左右どちらにも動かせない　● 左膝痛<br>● Neck Pain (Pain Spreading From Neck to Both Shoulders)<br>● Unable to Move Neck to Either Side　● Left Knee Pain |
| **使用した宝石**<br>Gemstones Used | ● キャッツアイ<br>● Cat's Eye |
| **ヒーリング前後の自覚症状の変化**<br>Changes in Perceived Symptoms Before and After Therapy | ピーンと走る痛み　Sharp Pain　　　　6 ➡ 0<br>重い痛み　Heavy Pain　　　　　　6 ➡ 0<br>引きつるような痛み　Tight, Pulling Pain　6 ➡ 0 |
| **その他の変化**<br>Other Changes | ● 全身の痛みが消え、首も左右に動かせるようになった<br>● Full-body pain disappeared, and neck can now move to both sides. |

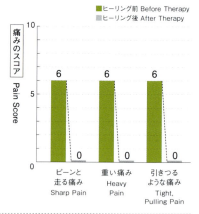

## Data 3　20代・女性　病名　アレルギー性鼻炎 (花粉症)
Female, 20s - Diagnosis: **Allergic Rhinitis** (Hay Fever)

| | |
|---|---|
| **特筆すべき症状、痛み**<br>Notable Symptoms or Pain | ● 鼻水　● 目のかゆみ　● 鼻づまり　● 喉のかゆみ<br>● Runny Nose　● Itchy Eyes<br>● Nasal Congestion　● Itchy Throat |
| **使用した宝石**<br>Gemstones Used | ● スペッサータイトガーネット　● デマントイドガーネット<br>● ドラゴンガーネット<br>● Spessartite Garnet　● Demantoid Garnet　● Dragon Garnet |
| **ヒーリング前後の自覚症状の変化**<br>Changes in Perceived Symptoms Before and After Therapy | 目のかゆみ　Itchy Eyes　　　　　　8 ➡ 0<br>鼻水　Runny Nose　　　　　　　8 ➡ 0<br>喉の違和感 (かゆみ)　Throat Discomfort (Itchiness)　10 ➡ 0 |
| **その他の変化**<br>Other Changes | ● 3分間の施術で花粉症の症状がすべて「0」まで改善し、3週間後も効果が継続している<br>● After a 3-minute treatment, all hay fever symptoms improved to "0," and the effects have lasted for 3 weeks. |

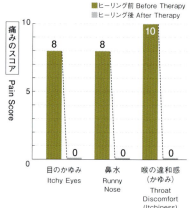

# 宝石種別効能リスト
## List of Benefits by Gemstone Type

宝石は種類によってそれぞれ違った効能があります。
今のあなたをサポートしてくれるのはどんな石なのか、
気になる石を探してみてください。

Each gemstone has its own unique benefits. Find the one that interests you and see which stone can support you right now.

## Red Stones
やる気と活力をもたらす情熱カラー
Passionate Colors that Boost Motivation and Vitality

### Ruby
ルビー

- 血流を促す
- 冷え症の改善
- 免疫力を高める
- 情熱を高める
- 若さを保つ

- Promotes blood circulation
- Helps relieve cold sensitivity
- Boosts immunity
- Enhances passion
- Supports youthful vitality

### Star Ruby
スタールビー

- 血流を促す
- 冷え性の改善
- 痛み、筋肉疲労などさまざまな身体的不調を改善する
- 運気を高める

- Promotes blood circulation
- Helps relieve cold sensitivity
- Eases pain, muscle fatigue, and other physical discomfort
- Brings good fortune

### Inca Rose
インカローズ

- 心の傷を癒す
- 愛情豊かになる
- 血流を促す
- 気持ちが明るくなる
- 元気が出る

- Heals emotional wounds
- Encourages love and compassion
- Promotes blood circulation
- Lifts the spirit
- Boosts energy

### Dragon Garnet
ドラゴンガーネット

- 不安、恐怖、怒り悲しみなどの苦しみを消し去る
- 心の苦しみ、ストレスに起因する様々な体の不調を改善する

- Relieves anxiety, fear, anger, and sadness
- Relieves physical discomfort linked to emotional stress

### Rubellite
ルベライト

- 喉の痛みの改善
- 気管支炎の改善
- 喘息の改善
- やる気を高める

- Relieves sore throat
- Improves bronchitis symptoms
- Eases asthma symptoms
- Boosts motivation

### Rhodolite Garnet
ロードライトガーネット

- マイナスエネルギーを取り去る
- リンパや血液の流れを促す
- 神経痛の緩和
- 精神を安定させる

- Removes negative energy
- Enhances lymphatic and blood flow
- Relieves nerve pain
- Calms the mind

※宝石ヒーリングの効果については、個人差がありますことをご了承ください
※ Please note that the effects of gemstone healing may vary from person to person

# 宝石種別効能リスト
List of Benefits by Gemstone Type

## Pink Stones
幸せを呼ぶ可憐で気品ある色
Sweet and Elegant Colors that Invite Happiness

### Pink Diamond
ピンクダイヤモンド

- 心身全体のエネルギーを高める
- 精神的に強くなる
- 他の宝石のエネルギーを高める
- Boosts overall energy of mind and body
- Strengthens mental resilience
- Enhances the energy of other gemstones

### Pink Sapphire
ピンクサファイア

- リンパや血液の流れを促す
- 低血圧や冷え性の改善
- 疲労感や肩こりを軽減
- 心が明るくなりポジティブになる
- Enhances lymphatic and blood flow
- Helps improve low blood pressure and alleviates cold sensitivity
- Relieves fatigue and shoulder stiffness
- Lifts the mood and promotes positivity

### Padparadscha Sapphire
パパラチアサファイア

- 気持ちが明るくなる
- 元気が出る
- 血液の流れを促す
- 美肌効果
- 低血圧の改善
- Lifts the spirit
- Boosts energy
- Promotes blood circulation
- Enhances skin health
- Helps improve low blood pressure

### Kunzite
クンツァイト

- 気持ちが明るくなる
- 気持ちをスッキリさせる
- 自信を与える
- リンパや血液の流れを促す
- Lifts the spirit
- Clears the mind
- Boosts confidence
- Enhances lymphatic and blood flow

### Morganite
モルガナイト

- ストレスでイライラした心を落ち着かせる
- 自律神経失調症の緩和
- うつ病の緩和
- 喜怒哀楽の感情をコントロール
- Calms a stressed and irritated mind
- Eases autonomic nervous system imbalances
- Alleviates depression
- Helps regulate emotions

### Diamond
ダイヤモンド

- 心身全体のエネルギーを高める
- 精神的に強くなる
- 他の宝石のエネルギーを高める
- Boosts overall energy of mind and body
- Strengthens mental resilience
- Enhances the energy of other gemstones

## White Stones
無垢な透明感がもたらす癒し
Healing through Pure and Clear Transparency

### Hyalite
ハイアライト

- 境界線を無限に広げる
- 魂の浄化
- Expands boundaries infinitely
- Purifies the soul

### Scapolite
スキャポライト

- カルマ、トラウマを取り去る
- 魂の浄化
- Releases karma and trauma
- Purifies the soul

# Orange Stones

暖色系の色がもたらす安心感
The Sense of Comfort from Warm Colors

### Orange Sapphire
オレンジサファイア

- 血流を促す
- 美肌効果で皮膚を若々しく保つ
- 気持ちが明るくなる
- 冷え性の改善
- 頭痛や鼻炎の緩和

- Promotes blood circulation
- Supports youthful skin with beautifying effects
- Lifts the spirit
- Alleviates cold sensitivity
- Relieves headaches and nasal inflammation

### Sphalerite
スファレライト

- 運気を高める
- 精神的に強くなる
- 耳鳴り、難聴の改善

- Brings good fortune
- Strengthens mental resilience
- Helps relieve tinnitus and hearing loss

### Spessartite Garnet
スペッサータイトガーネット

- 花粉症の緩和
- アトピーの緩和
- アレルギー性鼻炎の緩和

- Relieves hay fever
- Eases atopic dermatitis
- Alleviates allergic rhinitis

### Imperial Topaz
インペリアルトパーズ

- リンパや血液の流れを促す
- 心身のバランスを整える
- 婦人科系の不調の改善
- 精神を安定させる
- 心配、不安の解消

- Enhances lymphatic and blood flow
- Balances the mind and body
- Supports women's health
- Stabilizes the mind
- Eases worries and anxiety

### Yellow Sapphire
イエローサファイア

- 元気がでる
- 仕事の運気を高める
- 全体的な運気を高める

- Boosts energy
- Enhances career success
- Increases overall good fortune

# Yellow Stones

太陽のごとく人に希望と喜びを与える
Bringing Hope and Joy Like the Sun to Others

### Sphene
スフェーン

- 魂の浄化
- 精神的に強くなる

- Purifies the soul
- Strengthens mental resilience

### Cassiterite
キャシテライト

- 過去の戦いによって傷ついた心、魂を癒してくれる
- 心の不調に起因する身体的な不調の改善

- Heals the heart and soul wounded by past struggles
- Relieves physical discomfort linked to emotional stress

# 宝石種別効能リスト
List of Benefits by Gemstone Type

## Blue Stones
熱くなり過ぎた心を冷やし鎮静化
Calms and Cools an Overheated Mind

### Hauynite
アウイナイト

- 直感を高める
- 精神を安定させる
- 集中力を高める
- 心身のバランスを整える
- 自信と向上心を与える

- Enhances intuition
- Stabilizes the mind
- Improves focus
- Balances the mind and body
- Boosts confidence and ambition

### Apatite
アパタイト

- やる気を高める
- 精神を安定させる
- ストレスの緩和
- 心配、不安の解消

- Boosts motivation
- Stabilizes the mind
- Relieves stress
- Eases worries and anxiety

### Kyanite
カイヤナイト

- 精神を安定させる
- 潜在能力を高める
- 直観力を高める
- 心身のバランスを整える
- イライラを鎮める

- Stabilizes the mind
- Enhances potential
- Enhances intuition
- Balances the mind and body
- Calms irritability

### Sapphire
サファイア

- 精神を安定させる
- 高血圧の改善
- 芸術性を高める
- 集中力を高める

- Stabilizes the mind
- Helps improve high blood pressure
- Enhances artistic creativity
- Improves focus

### Stella Esperanza
ステラエスペランサ

- 魂の向上

- Elevates the Soul

### Paraiba Tourmaline
パライバトルマリン

- 原因不明の心身の不調の改善
- マイナスエネルギーの除去とブロック
- 頭痛の改善
- 風邪の緩和
- 胃腸の不調の緩和

- Alleviates unexplained physical and mental discomfort
- Removes and blocks negative energy
- Relieves headaches
- Eases cold symptoms
- Improves digestive discomfort

### Blue Zircon
ブルージルコン

- 幼い頃のトラウマを癒す
- 落ち着いて思考できるようになる
- 耳鳴りの改善

- Heals childhood trauma
- Promotes calm and clear thinking
- Helps relieve tinnitus

### Blue Spinel
ブルースピネル

- 心の闇を光に変える
- 精神を安定させる

- Transforms inner darkness into light
- Stabilizes the mind

### Royal Blue Moonstone
ロイヤルブルームーンストーン

- 精神を安定させる
- 安眠
- 直感力を高める
- イライラや怒りを鎮める
- 眼の疲れの緩和

- Stabilizes the mind
- Promotes restful sleep
- Enhances intuition
- Calms irritability and anger
- Relieves eye fatigue

# Purple Stones

感性をシャープに高めるインスピレーション
Inspiration that Sharpens and
Enhances Sensitivity

### Tanzanite
タンザナイト

- 運気を高める
- 精神を安定させる
- 芸術性を高める
- 耳鳴り、難聴の改善

- Brings good fortune
- Stabilizes the mind
- Enhances artistic creativity
- Helps relieve tinnitus and hearing loss

### Lavender Jade
ラベンダーヒスイ

- ストレスの緩和
- 強さを引き出す
- 胃腸・腎臓・肝臓の不調を緩和
- 運気を高める

- Relieves stress
- Enhances inner strength
- Supports stomach, kidney, and liver health
- Brings good fortune

### Hackmanite
ハックマナイト

- 精神的な強さを与える
- 心配・不安の解消
- 潜在能力を高める
- 血流を促す
- リンパの流れを促す

- Strengthens mental resilience
- Eases worries and anxiety
- Enhances potential
- Promotes blood circulation
- Supports lymphatic flow

# Multi color Stones

変幻自在の色の変化がもたらす特別な力
The Special Power Brought
by Ever-Changing Colors

### Alexandrite
アレキサンドライト

- 身体全般の不調改善
- 免疫力を高める
- 自信を与える

- Alleviates overall physical discomfort
- Boosts immunity
- Boosts confidence

### Color Change Fluorite
カラーチェンジフローライト

- 潜在能力を高める
- 気持ちが明るくなる
- ストレスを緩和する

- Enhances potential
- Lifts the spirit
- Relieves stress

### Ethiopian Opal
エチオピアオパール

- 心身のデトックス
- 肩こり、関節痛の緩和
- 神経痛の緩和
- 心身全体のエネルギーを高める
- 視界をクリアにする

- Detoxifies the mind and body
- Eases shoulder stiffness and joint pain
- Eases neuralgia
- Boosts overall energy of mind and body
- Clears vision

### Mexican Opal
メキシコオパール

- 婦人科系の不調を改善
- 眼の疲れの緩和
- 気持ちが明るくなる
- 元気が出る
- 関節痛、腰痛の緩和

- Supports women's health
- Relieves eye fatigue
- Lifts the spirit
- Boosts energy
- Eases joint pain and lower back pain

### Black Opal
ブラックオパール

- 骨の病気の改善
- 関節痛の緩和
- 腰痛の緩和
- 胃腸の不調の緩和
- 運気を高める

- Supports bone health
- Eases joint pain
- Relieves lower back pain
- Improves digestive discomfort
- Brings good fortune

宝石種別効能リスト
List of Benefits by Gemstone Type

# Green Stones

緑がもたらす安心感、穏やかな心
The Sense of Security and Calmness of Green

## Jade
ヒスイ

- 仕事運、金運などの運気を高める
- 胃腸の不調を改善する
- カルマの浄化

- Enhances career and financial fortune
- Improves digestive discomfort
- Purifies karma

## Emerald
エメラルド

- 眼の疲れの緩和
- 肩こりの改善
- 頭痛を改善
- 心身のバランスを整える
- 脊椎の矯正

- Relieves eye fatigue
- Eases shoulder stiffness
- Relieves headaches
- Balances the mind and body
- Supports spinal alignment

## Cat's Eye
キャッツアイ

- 運気を高める
- 自信を与える
- 向上心を高める

- Brings good fortune
- Boosts confidence
- Increases ambition

## Green Tourmaline
グリーントルマリン

- 胃腸の不調を緩和
- 精神を安定させる
- イライラや怒りを鎮める

- Improves digestive discomfort
- Stabilizes the mind
- Calms irritability and anger

## Green Garnet
グリーンガーネット

- 心身のバランスを整える
- 婦人科系の不調の改善
- 腰痛、肩こりの緩和
- 耳鳴り、難聴の改善
- 白内障や緑内障の改善

- Balances the mind and body
- Supports women's health
- Relieves lower back pain and shoulder stiffness
- Helps relieve tinnitus and hearing loss
- Aids in cataract and glaucoma relief

## Demantoid Garnet
デマントイドガーネット

- 肝臓、腎臓に働きかける
- 循環器系に作用する
- 利尿作用や解毒作用を高めてくれる
- 疲労からくる倦怠感からの回復

- Supports liver and kidney function
- Benefits the circulatory system
- Enhances diuretic and detoxifying effects
- Aids recovery from fatigue and exhaustion

## Pallasite Peridot
パラサイトペリドット

- 深いカルマを癒す
- 意識の次元を上昇させる
- ストレスの緩和

- Heals deep karma
- Elevates consciousness
- Relieves stress

## Peridot
ペリドット

- ストレスの緩和
- ネガティブな気持ちをなくす
- 気持ちの切り替え
- 肩こりの緩和
- 腰痛の緩和

- Relieves stress
- Reduces negative emotions
- Helps shift mindset
- Eases shoulder stiffness
- Alleviates lower back pain

## 自分に合った

# 宝石の見つけ方 &
# ヒーリング方法

Finding Your Perfect Gemstone & Healing Methods

**私たち人間も宝石も、それぞれ異なる波動を持っています。**
**自分の波動と共鳴し合い、健やかな状態に導いてくれる相性の良い宝石を探しましょう。**

Like us, gemstones each have their own unique vibrations. Find a gemstone that harmonizes with your energy and supports your well-being.

相性の合う宝石を見つけるためには、自分の感覚を信じ、感じてみることが重要です。気に入った宝石があったら、左の手のひらに載せ、何か感じるかどうか確かめてみてください。

右手ではなく左手を使うのは、エネルギーが左手から入って右手に抜ける性質があるためです。はじめは身構えてしまうかもしれませんが、力まず、心身ともリラックスした状態で行いましょう。温泉に入った時のように肩の力を抜き、ニュートラルな状態で宝石を感じてみましょう。

波動の合う宝石であれば、手が温かく感じられたり、指先がピリピリしたりします。感じ方はそれぞれいろいろあり、触れた瞬間にビビビと強く感じることもあれば、持っているうちに体が楽になることもあります。

宝石を載せた左手から10センチほど上に右手をかざすと、より感じやすくなります。温かさなどの感覚を得た場合は、宝石との波動が共鳴し合っている状態といえます。何も感じられない時、冷たく感じる時は、相性が合っていないのだと考えられます。

また、宝石店に並ぶ宝石のなかには、扱い方によってマイナスのエネルギーを吸い込んでいたり、エネルギーが弱くなっていたりするものもあります。自分自身の感覚でエネルギーを感じるかどうか試してみましょう。

To find a gemstone that aligns with your energy, trust your intuition and focus on how it feels. If you find a gemstone that interests you, place it on the palm of your left hand and see if you sense anything.

The reason for using your left hand instead of your right is that energy enters through the left hand and exits through the right. At first, you might feel tense, but try to relax both your body and mind. Just as when soaking in a hot bath, release any tension and allow yourself to connect with the gemstone in a neutral state.

If a gemstone's vibrations match yours, you may feel warmth in your hand or a tingling sensation in your fingertips. The way you perceive this connection varies—some people feel an instant, in-tense reaction the moment they touch a gemstone, while others gradually notice a sense of ease and relaxation as they hold it.

For a stronger connection, hover your right hand about 10 centimeters above the gemstone resting on your left hand. If you sense warmth or other sensations, it suggests that your vibrations are resonating with the gemstone. Conversely, if you feel nothing or the gemstone feels cold, it may not be the right match for you.

Additionally, some gemstones displayed in stores may have absorbed negative energy or weakened over time due to handling. Use your intuition to sense their energy and find the gemstone that truly resonates with you.

# Healing Methods

ヒーリングメソッド

## 左手で宝石を握る
### Hold the Gemstone in Your Left Hand

ルースでも、指輪、ペンダントなどでも同じ。宝石を左の手のひらに載せ、包み込むように軽く握り、5〜10分ほど目を閉じてリラックスします。椅子などに腰かけた姿勢で行うとよいでしょう。ベッドに横になってもかまいません。

Place the gemstone in the palm of your left hand, gently close your fingers around it, and relax with your eyes closed for 5 to 10 minutes. Sitting in a chair is ideal, but lying down on a bed is also fine. This method applies whether it's a loose gemstone, a ring, or a pendant.

## 患部に直接宝石を貼る
### Place the gemstone directly on the affected area.

胃痛なら胃、肩こりなら痛みを感じる肩の部分に、医療用のテープで直接、宝石を貼ります。体を動かして宝石をなくさないように十分注意してください。

If you have a stomachache, place the gemstone directly on your stomach. For shoulder stiffness, attach it to the area where you feel pain using medical tape. Be careful not to lose the gemstone when moving around.

## 他の人にヒーリングしてもらう
### Receive Healing from Someone Else

家族や友人など親しい人にお願いするといいでしょう。ただし、心身ともに健康な人である必要があります。ヒーリングを施す人が宝石を左手に持ち、右の手のひらを患部にかざします。ヒーリングを受ける人は、目を閉じてリラックスします。

It is best to ask a close family member or friend. However, the person performing the healing should be in good physical and mental health. The healer holds the gemstone in their left hand and hovers their right palm over the affected area. The person receiving the healing should close their eyes and relax.

　相性の合う宝石を見つけたら、そのエネルギーを最大限に享受するためには、身に着ける場所、そしてどのようなデザインにするかも重要です。

　気に入った宝石を指輪にするか、ペンダントにするか迷った場合は、胸元に置いた時と指に置いた時の感覚の違いをチェックします。さらに、指輪をどの指につけるかは、左右十指の付け根にそれぞれ宝石を置いてみて、一番エネルギーを感じる指を見極めて決めます。

　次に、デザインです。その石に合うデザインにすると、本来の力をさらに引き出すことができます。デザイン枠やデザイン画の上に宝石を置き、上から左手をかざして温かさなどエネルギーを感じるかどうか確かめましょう。ダイヤモンドなどほかの宝石と組み合わせることで、相乗効果が得られることもあります。

　宝石店にはデザインがすでに施された空枠（枠の見本）がある場合もあり、中石を置いてみると、イメージを固めるのに役立ちます。うまくマッチする空枠が見つかれば、それを利用してセミオーダーで作ることができます。

　日常生活において、相性の合う宝石をヒーリングに活用する場合、左ページに示したような方法をとることができます。

Once you find a gemstone that resonates with you, it is important to consider where to wear it and what design to choose to fully benefit from its energy.

If you are unsure whether to set your gemstone in a ring or a pendant, try placing it on your chest and then on your finger to compare how each feels. To determine which finger to wear a ring on, place the gemstone at the base of each finger on both hands and see where you sense the strongest energy.

Next, consider the design. Choosing a design that suits the stone can further enhance its natural energy. To test this, place the gemstone on different design settings or sketches, then hover your left hand above it to sense any warmth or energy. Combining the stone with other gems, such as diamonds, may also create a synergistic effect.

Some jewelry stores offer pre-designed empty settings. By placing the center stone in one of these settings, you can get a clearer image of the final piece. If you find a setting that matches well, you can have it made as a semi-custom order.

For incorporating your gemstone into daily healing practices, refer to the methods described on the left page.

# 宝石のお手入れ方法

## How to Care for Gemstones

**宝石本来のエネルギーを上手に活用するためには、
その石がきちんと浄化され、クリアな状態であることが重要です。**

To effectively harness a gemstone's natural energy,
it is essential to ensure that the stone is properly cleansed and energetically clear.

宝石を身に着けたり、エネルギーを活用するために手に持ったりすると、自然と汗や脂がつきます。せっかくのエネルギーが弱くなったりしないように、日頃から愛情をもってお手入れを行い、クリアな状態を保つようにしましょう。

指輪やペンダントを身に着けた後は、なるべくその日のうちに汗や汚れなどを洗い流します。右ページで説明した方法のように、宝石専用の洗浄・浄化剤であるクリアリングエッセンスを使うと効果的です。小まめにお手入れを行うと、宝石の輝きは増します。指輪やペンダントの側面、裏面、メレダイヤの間など、汚れがたまりやすい部分を中心に優しくブラッシングしましょう。毛先の柔らかい歯ブラシを使用して、宝石の表面はそっとなでるだけにとどめます。

ただし、エチオピアオパール、ステラエスペランサ、ロードナイト、ハックマナイト、フローライト、真珠やトルコ石などは水に弱いため、水で洗い流すのは避けましょう。これらについては、宝石専用の浄化剤であるクリアリングミストで浄化する方法があります。

宝石の浄化は、宝石のエネルギーをリセットし、活性化させることを意味しています。ヒーリング効果を持続させるには、使用するごとに浄化することが大切。右ページの方法で水を取り替えた後、宝石の周りに気泡がつくようならまだ浄化が終わっていないしるしです。気泡がつかなくなるまで浄化を繰り返します。

When you wear a gemstone or hold it to harness its energy, it naturally accumulates sweat and oils. To prevent its energy from weakening, it is important to care for it regularly with love and attention, keeping it in a clear and purified state.

After wearing a ring or pendant, try to cleanse it the same day to remove sweat and dirt. Using a specialized gemstone cleansing solution, such as Clearing Essence (described on the right page), can be particularly effective. Regular maintenance enhances the stone's brilliance. Focus on areas where dirt tends to accumulate, such as the sides and back of rings and pendants or between melee diamonds. Use a soft-bristled toothbrush and gently brush the gemstone's surface.

However, some stones—such as Ethiopian opal, Stella Esperanza, rhodonite, hackmanite, fluorite, pearls, and turquoise—are sensitive to water and should not be washed. Instead, cleanse them using a gemstone-specific purifier, like Clearing Mist.

Cleansing a gemstone helps reset and revitalize its energy. To maintain its healing effects, it is important to purify it after each use. After replacing the water as described on the right page, check if bubbles form around the gemstone. If bubbles appear, the cleansing process is not yet complete. Repeat the process until no bubbles remain.

## Cleansing

### 宝石を洗浄する
### Cleansing the Gemstone

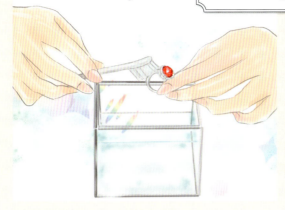

宝石にクリアリングエッセンス、または中性洗剤（台所用食器洗剤）を数的垂らし、柔らかい毛先の歯ブラシで全体を軽くブラッシングします。ルースは手のひらに載せ、優しく洗います。誤って宝石を排水口に流さないように栓をするなど注意してください。

Apply a few drops of Clearing Essence or a neutral detergent (such as dish soap) to the gemstone, then gently brush it all over with a soft-bristled toothbrush. For loose gemstones, place them in the palm of your hand and wash them gently. Make sure to plug the drain or take precautions to prevent the gemstone from accidentally slipping down the sink.

### 宝石を浄化する
### Purifying the Gemstone

## Purifying

透明な器に水を入れ、宝石を入れます。クリアリングエッセンスを5〜6滴垂らして40分ほど置きます（中性洗剤の場合は6時間）。その後、水を取り替え、エッセンスを入れずに40分つけておきます。宝石の周りに気泡がつく場合、最初の工程から再び行います。

Fill a clear container with water and place the gemstone inside. Add 5 to 6 drops of Clearing Essence and let it sit for about 40 minutes (or 6 hours if using a neutral detergent). Then, replace the water and soak the gemstone for another 40 minutes without adding Clearing Essence.If bubbles form around the gemstone, restart the process from the beginning.

## Purifying

### 水に弱い宝石を浄化する
### Purifying Water-Sensitive Gemstone

ティッシュを手に取り、30センチ以上離れたところからクリアリングミストを1回吹きかけます。ミストをかけたのとは反対の面を内側にして宝石をふわっとくるみ、15分ほど置いておきます。

Take a tissue and spray Clearing Mist once from a distance of at least 30 centimeters. Wrap the gemstone loosely with the misted side outward, and let it sit for about 15 minutes.

177

ギンザベルエトワール
Belle Etoile Co., Ltd.

東京都中央区銀座7-10-5　4F　☎ (03) 3289-5718
4F 7-10-5,Ginza,Chuo-ku,Tokyo　+81-3-3289-5718

Email mail@belleetoile.co.jp
https://www.belleetoile.co.jp/

監修者プロフィール

**岡本 敬人** TAKAHITO OKAMOTO

株式会社ベル・エトワール代表取締役社長／
ジュエリーエネルギーアドバイザー

多くの人を笑顔にしたいという思いのもと音楽活動を行い、1997年にバンドのヴォーカリストとしてメジャーデビュー。音楽業界の第一線で多岐に渡って活躍する。2010年に株式会社ベル・エトワールの創業者であり宝石の伝道師の岡本憲将氏と出会い、宝石が持つ癒しの力に感銘を受け、自身もその価値を多くの人に伝えたいと憲将氏に師事し、2012年にジュエリーエネルギーアドバイザーの資格を取得。これまでに2万人以上の宝石フィッティングを行う。2017年より株式会社ベル・エトワールの代表取締役を引き継ぎ、東京・銀座を拠点に全国でセミナーや体感会を開催。著書に『宝石の常識 永久保存版』(双葉社)、『JEWELLNESS 心と体を癒す宝石の価値』(幻冬舎MC)、『Gemstone 人々を輝かせる宝石の秘密』(幻冬舎MC)がある。

Supervised by
**Takahito Okamoto**

President & CEO of Belle Etoile Co., Ltd. /
Jewelry Energy Advisor

Driven by a passion for bringing joy to people, Mr.Takahito Okamoto first pursued a career in music, making his major debut as a band vocalist in 1997. He thrived in the music industry, engaging in a wide range of creative and professional activities.In 2010, he met Mr. Kensho Okamoto, the founder of Belle Etoile Co., Ltd. and a renowned gemstone evangelist. Deeply moved by the healing energy of gemstones, he decided to study under Mr. Okamoto to share this knowledge with a wider audience. In 2012, he obtained certification as a Jewelry Energy Advisor and has since conducted gemstone fittings for over 20,000 individuals.In 2017, he took over as president & CEO of Belle Etoile Co., Ltd. Based in Ginza, Tokyo, he organizes seminars and experiential gemstone events across Japan. He is also the author of *Basic Knowledge of Gemstones: The Ultimate Guide* (Futabasha Publishers Ltd.), *JEWELLNESS: The Healing Energy of Gemstones* (Gentosha Media Consulting), and *Gemstone: The Secret to Enhancing People's Brilliance* (Gentosha Media Consulting).

---

宝石の常識 International
（ほうせき の じょうしき インターナショナル）
2025年4月19日　第1刷発行

| | |
|---|---|
| 監　修 | 岡本敬人（おかもとたかひと） |
| 発行人 | 島野浩二 |
| 発行所 | 株式会社双葉社 |

〒162-8540
東京都新宿区東五軒町3番28号
☎ (03)5261-4818（営業）　☎ (03)5261-4869（編集）
https://www.futabasha.co.jp/
（双葉社の書籍・コミック・ムックがご購入いただけます）

印刷・製本　TOPPANクロレ株式会社

※落丁、乱丁の場合は送料双葉社負担でお取り替えいたします。「製作部」宛にお送りください。ただし、古書店で購入したものについてはお取り替えできません。
☎(03)5261-4822（製作部）
※定価はカバーに表示してあります。
※本書のコピー、スキャン、デジタル化等の無断複製・転載は著作権法上の例外を除き禁じられています。本書を代行業者等の第三者に依頼してスキャンやデジタル化することは、たとえ個人や家庭内での利用でも著作権法違反です。

©Takahito Okamoto 2025 Printed in Japan
ISBN978-4-575-31967-5 C0076

- Edited by Yukika Mitsumoto（光元志佳／株式会社クラリス）
  　　　　　 Teruhisa Tanimizu（谷水輝久／株式会社双葉社）
- Written by Shizuko Mitsuhashi（三橋志津子）
- Photo by Mikiro Tamai（玉井幹郎）
- Translation by Hideka Shinohara（篠原求佳）
- Illustration by maya'chi
- Design by Hiroki Odawara（小田原宏樹）
- Produced by Akiko Okamoto［Belle Etoile Co., Ltd］
  （岡本明子／株式会社ベル・エトワール）